Joy Breaks

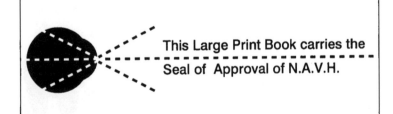

This Large Print Book carries the
Seal of Approval of N.A.V.H.

Joy Breaks

90 Devotions to
Celebrate, Simplify,
and Add Laughter
to Your Life.

Patsy Clairmont
Barbara Johnson
Marilyn Meberg
Luci Swindoll

✗❤✗❤✗❤✗❤✗❤✗❤✗❤✗❤✗❤✗❤

with Traci Mullins

Walker Large Print • Waterville, Maine

Scripture quotations are from:
The Holy Bible, New International Version (NIV), © 1973, 1984 by the International Bible Society. Used by permission of Zondervan Publishing House;
New American Standard Bible (NASB), © 1960, 1977 by the Lockman Foundation;
The New King James Version (NKJV), © 1984 by Thomas Nelson, Inc.;
The King James Version (KJV);
The Living Bible (TLB), © 1971 by Tyndale House Publishers;
The Message, © 1993 by Eugene H. Peterson;
The Revised Standard Version Bible (RSV), © 1946, 1952, 1971 by the Division of Christian Education of the National Council of Churches of Christ in the USA.
Used by permission.

Published in 2002 by arrangement with Zondervan Publishing House, a division of HarperCollins.

The text of this Large Print edition is unabridged.
Other aspects of the book may vary from the original edition.

Set in 16 pt. Plantin by Christina S. Huff.

Printed in the United States on permanent paper.

Library of Congress Control Number: 2002110747
ISBN 1-4104-0040-9 (lg. print : sc : alk paper)

CONTENTS

Odd Ducks in Silk Hats:
Relishing the Peculiar

Present Tensions:
Savoring Your Moments

Giggle Breaks:
Practicing a Laugh Life-style

A Little Joyboost

A Mouthful of Laughter

Barbara Johnson

He will yet fill your mouth with laughter
and your lips with shouts of joy.

JOB 8:21

At some time in life every woman will ask,
"What will keep me young?" Is the secret of
youth different for everyone, or is there some
universal antiaging potion?

I heard someone say recently that *laughter*
is her drug of choice. Simple as that.
Laughter is the language of the young at
heart and the antidote to what ails us. No
drugstore prescription is required; laughter
is available to anyone at any time. Laughter's benefits are felt immediately. With
large doses, the benefits show on our face, in
our body language, and in the spring in our
step. So who needs a face-lift or crazy diets
that don't work?

Did you know that one laugh burns six calories? Laughing is jogging for your insides. It increases heart rate and circulation, stimulates the immune system, and improves the muscle tone of the abdomen. Dr. William Fry of Stanford University says laughing heartily a hundred times a day has the same beneficial effects as ten minutes on a rowing machine.

According to *Psychology Today* magazine, laughter goes hand in hand with creativity, too. Researchers found that people with a keen sense of humor have a more creative outlook to problem solving than do somber individuals. Tests also showed those who had listened to a comedy album were able to withstand twenty percent more pain than those tested who were not exposed to humor. Other studies show that companies encouraging employees to bring a sense of humor to work are more profitable than those emphasizing business-as-usual. If these facts are true, we should be laughing on a grand scale in everything we do and using laughter as a barometer of success.

If you want to get to know someone, I say: *Don't bother analyzing the way she talks or what her ambitions and ideals may be. Just watch her laugh.* If I were an employer, I'd hire the person who laughs well. If I were a single woman, I'd marry the man who laughs well. If I were looking for a special friend, I'd search until I met a woman who laughs well.

God gave us this capacity to be tickled way deep down inside. Giggles are as contagious as a viral disease. And y'know what? You don't have to be happy to laugh. You become happy *because* you laugh.

One day when my boys were little I came home from shopping and heard all four of them in the kitchen shrieking with hilarity. They were flicking huge spoonfuls of gooey raspberry Jell-O with bananas against a white wall at the far end of the kitchen and watching it ooze down to the floor.

I walked in and asked nonchalantly, "Where's my spoon?"

Tim promptly grabbed a soup ladle and handed it to me. I loaded it with a glob of goo and fired off. It hit the wall with a giant splat. Hey, this *was* fun! I started to laugh, scooped up another load, and let it fly. My boys joined in, and soon the wall was a red dripping mess. We were laughing hysterically — yes, even two hours later as they finished scrubbing the wall and cleaning up the floor.

Today, I wonder if my two oldest boys are laughing in heaven. I think they must be cooking up all kinds of jokes and games around the throne of God. And as for the rest of us here on earth, I think about how the many hours of laughter we shared with Tim and Steve helped prepare us for their deaths. Laughter is to life what shock absorbers are to automobiles. It won't take the potholes out of the road, but it sure makes the ride smoother.

When the losses of life became unbearable for me, I coped and learned to move on by cultivating a sense of humor. Later, seeing everything in a humorous light became a way of life to dissolve disappointment. It works every time. One day when I ran into a high school classmate I realized she had aged so much she didn't even recognize me! (See how humor turns everything around?)

There is nothing like a mouthful of laughter. Get some for yourself and everyone else you know.

"Dear Lord Jesus, I would have loved to hear the sound of your laughter ringing through the Galilean hills. I'm sure it was a rich, warm sound that made other people want to hang around you. Help me spread your love through chuckles and smiles to as many people as possible today. Amen."

GIMME A BREAK

Enjoying Life's Perks

HELP . . . NOW!

Patsy Clairmont

O LORD, come quickly to help me.

PSALM 70:1

Do you ever just want to throw back your
head and bellow, "Gimme a break"? Life has
a way of mounting up until we are slumping
down. Soon our joyful noises turn into
grumpy groans.

Well, we are not alone. For I hear
whimperings of men, women, the rich, the
poor, the young, and the old echo
throughout the pages of Scripture. You may
not find them using the phrase, "Gimme a
break," but some of their verbiage vibrates
with attitude. That attitude proclaims, "I've
had enough, I've gone far enough, I've given
way too much, and I'm not doing this anymore."

I noticed the Israelites wanted a break
from their monotonous manna menu.

Sautéed or flambéed, the historical Tony-the-Tiger-like flakes were making the weary wayfarers hysterical. Day in, day out, the manna fell from heaven, and Mom served the same old sweet-tasting food. Why, the Israelites finally became so disgruntled they even wanted to backtrack to Egypt to chow down on smelly leeks and stinky onions. I guess they thought halitosis was better than one more helping of Mama's manna.

Then there was Sarah, wife of Abraham. Seems she was fed up with her servant girl Hagar and Hagar's son, Ishmael. This was the second blowup between Sarah and the hired help; only this time Sarah wanted a permanent break from the pair. (Ever felt that way about someone?) She wanted Hagar and Ishmael out of her face, her family, and her fortune. So Abraham complied with Sarah's wishes and sent the pair packing with only the barest of essentials: bread and water.

Speaking of water, I wonder during Noah's boat-building days if his wife ever needed a break from his constant ark involvement? Scripture doesn't tell us her reaction to those years, but I can imagine, if she was anything like us, that she, too, must have thought, "C'mon, enough is enough! Gimme a break." The desire for an intermission must have multiplied when they were actually bobbing atop mountain peaks with their rowdy cargo.

I watch young moms board airplanes (arks) toting babies and all the endless, yet necessary, paraphernalia (cargo), and I wonder how they do it. I do catch glimpses of their frayed nerves and exhaustion, and I sometimes see in their eyes neon signs that flash, "Gimme a break . . . please!"

I'm not sure David said "please," but I do hear him plead frequently in the Psalms for a reprieve from his enemies. Check out Psalm 70:1, 5: "Hasten, O God, to save me; O LORD, come quickly to help me. . . . You are my help and my deliverer; O LORD, do not delay."

David needed a break *now*. He was pleading with the Lord of the universe to drop everything else he was doing and rescue him. *Now* is usually when I need my help as well. That's because I tend to let things — activities, demands, mail, dishes, bills, laundry, telephone messages, people's expectations — pile up until I'm howling for help and blubbering the blues.

Jonah was a fellow who sure understood blubbering. In fact, he was taking a sea sabbatical when he found himself encased in blubber. Jonah took a self-appointed break, and it almost broke him. Once on land again it wasn't long before he was back in blubber; this time it was his own, as he wailed and whined that life and people were so difficult he wanted a permanent break. As a matter of fact, he just wanted to die.

It's obvious that, as long as we can find a reflection in the mirror, we will long for a break. And that's not wrong. Many times it's imperative if we're to avoid breaking. But other times, when we reach the end of our strength, wisdom, and personal resources, we enter into the beginning of his glorious provisions. And that's a wondrous place to be.

"Dear Lord, like a child with her mom, when I say now, *I mean* right now! *Thank you for not always dropping everything in the universe and rushing to my rescue. Instead, you have allowed me to feel my neediness and experience my limitations so I will understand that it is you who will (eventually) save me. I don't want to refuse your perfect plan; I want to find refuge in you. Then I will have the stamina to make it to the end. Amen."*

Don't Grin and Bear It

Barbara Johnson

Those who sow in tears will reap with songs of joy. He who goes out weeping, carrying seed to sow, will return with songs of joy, carrying sheaves with him.

PSALM 126:5–6

You can tell it's going to be a rotten day when

- you call suicide prevention and they put you on hold.
- you put your bikini top on backward and it fits better.
- your blind date turns out to be your ex-boyfriend.

But just remember, every flower that ever bloomed had to go through a whole lot of dirt to get there! And with the dirt, a lot of watering was needed.

Scientific research indicates that tears — real, wet, human tears — may be the body's

17

mechanism for flushing away harmful chemicals produced during stress. A study at Harvard University showed that people who cried more in response to grief were less likely to suffer heart attacks after losing a loved one. (Previous studies showed that the risk of suffering a heart attack after such a loss is fourteen times greater than normal.) Imagine: tears can break the chain of chemical events that lead to heart disease and brain damage.

Crying is the only physiological process experienced by humans that animals do not share. Crying tears makes us human in the finest sense of the word. Doctors now say shedding tears is one of the most effective performances of the human body. And there are many uneducated people who know the therapeutic value of a good old-fashioned cry: sobbing, wailing, howling, just letting it all out.

You don't have to grin and bear it. You don't have to be holier-than-thou, keeping up a "spiritual" front that equates tears with weakness and doubt. No, scientists now confirm what the Bible has said for thousands of years: tears are God's gift to his precious children. When we cry, we allow our bodies to function according to God's design — and we embrace one of the "perks" he offers to relieve our stress.

Someone said, "God will accept a broken heart, but he must have all the pieces." As he stitches those pieces back together, the moisture of tears softens and makes flexible his strong thread of healing in our lives. Big wet tears are part of the rich human experience. The people who weep unashamed are the same ones who live and love with their whole heart and soul. Those who mourn are those who have allowed themselves to feel real feelings because they care about other people.

Do you realize what a gift it is to feel, even if it hurts? Many people do not allow themselves the privilege of being happy or sad. Some think courage is synonymous with stoicism. But God does not hand out medals for *not crying*. King David wrote in Psalm 34:4: "I sought the LORD, and he answered me; he delivered me from all my fears [not *tears*]."

I have a friend who cried buckets of tears through a divorce. She struggled with rage and anger, then felt guilty about her feelings. Her prayers most often consisted of simply releasing her pain by crying it out. During one such deluge of tears, she realized the rage she felt toward her ex-husband's betrayal was a reflection of how deeply she had loved him. Her tears dissolved her guilt. They were a vehicle to accept and then release honest emotion.

Sometimes allowing yourself to cry is the scariest thing you'll ever do. And the bravest. It takes a lot of courage to face the facts, stare loss in the face, bare your heart, and let it bleed. But it is the only way to cleanse your wounds and prepare them for healing. God will take care of the rest.

"Father, thank you for providing a way for us to release the pressure of stress and grief in a healthy way. May our tears soften the way for your glory in our lives and create streams in our deserts. Amen."

THE BEST-LAID PLANS

Patsy Clairmont

The LORD is near to all who call on him.

PSALM 145:18

I'm afraid my husband took this thought, "Gimme a break," a little too literally. Last week he fell in our kitchen and suffered a triple fracture to his ankle. Now he is in a cast, on crutches, and is definitely taking a break as well as having one. Whereas I, who thought I was going to take a break from a busy year of travel and speaking, find myself galloping around our premises caring for my beloved . . . hand and, yep, foot.

Now don't get me wrong; I'm grateful to be Les's nurse. I wouldn't want to be anywhere but with him. It's just that life takes so many unexpected twists and turns right in the middle of some of our best-laid plans. We had moved two weeks before Les's fall, and we both had high expectations of how we would settle into our new abode. Now our teamwork has turned into me-work. To tell you the truth, I'm not that handy.

I think the first sign that we were in for some interesting days, with Les laid up and me at the helm, was minutes after his fall. Our friend Dan was coming to assist our son Marty in maneuvering my injured husband to the car. Marty suggested I turn on the porch light for Dan's arrival. I dashed to the front door, and instead of turning on the light, I rang the doorbell. No, I can't tell you why I did that. Panicked? Possibly. Menopausal? Definitely. Space cadet? Precisely.

Since Les broke his right ankle, I have become the designated driver. Oh, boy, Les has been waiting for this chance — payback time for years of my advising him how to drive. Before I even got out of our yard for our first visit to the doctor, I came under Les's tutelage. Our new home has a rather long driveway that I have to back out of, and I'm not a back-up kind of woman. I'm more your full-speed-ahead kind of gal. My car's backseat window ledge is designed too high for me to see to back up, so I have to rely on my side mirrors. For some reason I can't stay on a straight-mirrored course, and we looked like a Weeble. (You know, those round-bottomed toys children have that wobble all over.) I was in the flower beds, then off the other side brushing the tree trunks, and then back over to the grass and onto the sidewalk before finally reaching the road. Les was amazed. Well, amazed might be understating his response. I watched as concern spread across his face (like hives). He seemed to realize he had several months of these yard exits to live through — and so does the yard.

Not only am I not great at backing up, but I'm also not that impressive at climbing up. Yet up is where I needed to go to pound the nails in the brackets to hold the curtains in the living room. Les looked pale as he observed me ascending the ladder. I assured him I could handle this task. But when I attempted to pound the itsy-bitsy nail into the wood, I dropped the bracket. I scampered down, scaled back up, and promptly dropped the hammer. Down the ladder I scurried again, grabbed the hammer, and made my way back up to the ceiling . . . huffing and puffing. (This was more aerobic than a StairMaster.) After the third drop (this time it was the nail), Les's head also dropped as he slowly shook it back and forth. Okay, okay, Bob Vila I'm not.

Although I did try a Vila-approach in our bathroom. I wanted to hang a cupboard that was heavy, and Les said I would have to nail it into the studs. One night I began to thump on the wall trying to detect the sound difference between wallboard and wood (as if I would know). Les heard my Morse code taps and jogged in on his crutches to prevent me from inadvertently ripping out a wall with my cupboard. O ye of little faith.

Les then sent me to the store to buy a stud finder so we could "do it right." I made my way to the hardware department but couldn't locate the stud finders. Two men were working in that department, but I was hesitant to ask them because I was concerned they would think I was being fresh. Finally I blurted out, "Where are your stud finders?" They smiled. They knew where they were, but they couldn't figure out how they worked or what size batteries they needed. (That made me feel a lot better.)

Then I had them direct me to the toggle screws. I needed one, only one, to mount the toilet-paper holder. Uncertain which of the three thousand screws was correct, I purchased thirty-five of them to improve my odds of "doing it right." Yep, you guessed it: they were all wrong.

C'mon, folks, gimme a break. I'm the one with a loose screw if I think I can do all these unnatural tasks. (Although I now know how to identify a stud finder and what kind of batteries it takes. I can even operate the thing.) I'm doing better backing the car out of the driveway, and with the exception of our glider, a tree, and several flowers, I've hardly rammed into anything. I've also learned when I need to put up curtain brackets to call Bob Vila. And when I need a break, even in the midst of twists and turns, to call upon the Lord.

"Thank you, Lord Jesus, for hearing my cry and for walking me through my slips and falls. Amen."

CALMING FAITH

Patsy Clairmont

He maketh me to lie down
in green pastures: he leadeth
me beside the still waters.

PSALM 23:2 (kjv)

The sweet psalmist David sang of calming faith. Lean in and listen to a line of this beloved recital: "He maketh me to lie down in green pastures: he leadeth me beside the still waters."

Notice David sang of how the Lord "maketh" and the Lord "leadeth." In other words, young David didn't come up with the idea to stop and rest in the lush pastureland. His youthful vitality probably vied for higher ground. David was probably humming bee-bop, and the Lord was saying, "Stop." The Lord knew that the shepherd boy and the sheep needed a break.

David then points out that he had to be led by the Lord to the still waters. I wonder if

David had to be led because he was naturally drawn to the excitement of the rushing waters? It certainly is that way with us. Left to our own agendas, we either run at breakneck speeds right past the pasture, enamored with our frenzied pace, or sit in parched misery. The Shepherd, who understands our naiveté and our humanity (not to mention our sheeplike stupidity), intervenes on our behalf to guide us with a strong hand onto a quiet path and into a calmer faith.

Yep, a calmer faith. That's the quiet place within us where we don't get whiplash every time life tosses us a curve. Where we don't revolt when his plan and ours conflict. Where we relax (versus stew, sweat, and swear) in the midst of an answerless season. Where we accept (and expect) deserts in our spiritual journey as surely as we do joy. Where we are not intimidated or persuaded by other people's agendas but moved only by him. Where we weep in repentance, sleep in peace, live in fullness, and sing of victory.

Ultimately our life in Christ makes us winners. And being winners in the Lord means that nothing we go through is for naught. There is just something about knowing that my failures, others' failures, hardships, mistakes, losses, and pain have meaning. For me, that understanding eases some of the agony of life and encourages me to keep on keeping on.

If you asked those who know me well, they would tell you I am a reactive woman. Often overstated in my responses, I have knots on my cranium from bouncing off ceilings. I've always admired laid-back people (when I wasn't aggravated by their seeming lack of gumption). I know I need to settle down, but I'm wired tightly. Even though some of those wires seem frayed (like the ones that connect my thoughts), I can't nestle down in the green pastures long enough to enjoy the feast of his provision. It's also difficult for me to stay at the water's edge to quench my thirst because I'm busy splashing around in the shallowness of my own agenda. Imagine giving up Niagara Falls for a dripping faucet.

I'm grateful the Lord maketh and the Lord leadeth, for I needeth in a big way! I needeth the One who madeth me to holdeth me together. When I am irrational, irksome, or irate, I need the Shepherd of this willful sheep to maketh me still and sane. That way, instead of telling off tellers, I can extend courtesy. Instead of setting my husband straight, I can extend understanding. Instead of having all the answers, I can extend a listening ear.

Perhaps that is why the Lord brought David to the pasture and the water's edge. He knew this young boy would one day be an influential king, and he would need to know how to be still, understanding, attentive, courteous, and calm. The Lord knew David would have to deal with critical issues both politically and personally. He knew the king would need to know where to go when life became too much, when he needed to be restored in his soul, when he just plain needed a break.

When you need a break, where do you tend to go? The mountains? A valley? A pastureland? The water's edge?

Wherever each of us chooses, we all know what it feels like to be at rest. And we all long for that more sane life-style rather than being overwhelmed. But are we willing to leave the press long enough to lie down in the soothing green pastures and to be led by the still waters of his provision? That, my friend, is not resort living but restored living. And each of us needs it.

"Thank you, Lord, for your strong hand lest I miss the resting places and the water's edge. For there you help me to understand some of

life's mystery, and you restore my languid soul. I ask you to still my frantic heart and calm my shaky faith in Jesus' name. Amen."

CROAKINGS OF JOY

Marilyn Meberg

Let me hear joy and gladness.

PSALM 51:8

Now that I'm living in the desert in a condominium, I haven't been in such close proximity to other people since dorm life in college. And frankly, I love it! I like to be surrounded by people; I like to hear occasional plumbing sounds, human voices, and even know what my neighbors are watching on TV. (I don't always approve of their choices, but I suppose people have the right to be wrong on occasion.) I find all this closeness rather comforting. Plus I've also gotten some wonderful giggles as a result.

For example, my neighbors to the left (Bob and Julie) are warm, sociable people who love to laugh and entertain. Several days ago I noticed through the window (the window is directly behind my desk so I occasionally swivel around just to keep in touch)

31

that Bob was putzing around with a mechanical green frog that is supposed to croak when you get within two feet of it. It continues to croak until you leave its "croak space."

Apparently, this frog was not performing properly and in exasperation Bob called into the house to Julie, "This frog has truly croaked . . . it won't make a sound." I smiled at this clever pun and swiveled back to work.

Yesterday my friend Pat came over with her little dachshund, Mr. Hobbs, to go on our scheduled walk. As we came out the front door, Mr. Hobbs noticed Bob's green frog on the front stoop. Hobbs bristled, did his deep-throated growl (which never sounds threatening . . . he must hate that) and stealthily crept toward it. Not knowing that Bob had replaced the mechanically dead croaker with one that functioned, I was as startled as Mr. Hobbs when it started croaking loudly. Hobbs jumped straight into the air and dashed behind Pat for safety.

Last night, returning from a wild and woolly night at the movies, I made my uncertain way in the dark to my front door. I'd forgotten to leave the porch light on and apparently entered the croak zone unawares because my presence set the frog into a frenzy of croaking which did not stop until I got inside. I giggled to myself as I realized I would never be able to sneak in and out of my own house as long as this vigilant green frog was on duty.

This frog provides me with yet another example of my theory that the giggles in life usually come from little things. If we train ourselves to look for them, see them, and then giggle with them or even at them, we get a "perk." Seeing these potential breaks from routine sometimes requires that we adjust the lenses through which we see life. That adjustment can be as simple as heightening our awareness of the quirky and unusual around us. Giggle potential is everywhere; we just need to slow down long enough to see it.

"Lord Jesus, without our knowledge of you and salvation from you, we would be unable to truly 'hear joy' or feel gladness. You are the source of our peace, the foundation upon which our security rests, and the inspiration for finding gladness in the dailyness of our lives. May we experience more God-given gladness as we celebrate the days you have ordained for us here on earth. Amen."

TEN THOUSAND BUTTERFLIES — MAYBE MORE

Marilyn Meberg

How many are your works, O LORD!
In wisdom you made them all;
the earth is full of your creatures.

PSALM 104:24

Last week I got one of those delicious "life perks" while driving to "Parents' Place" in Pacific Grove, California. Before I describe my perk, let me fill you in on a couple of tidbits of information.

My daughter, Beth, her golf pro husband, Steve, and my adorable seventeen-month-old grandson, Ian, live in Carmel, California (a very long nine-hour drive from Grandma). Ever since Ian was six days old, Beth and he have gone to the neighboring town of Pacific Grove for a weekly meeting of moms and

34

their little ones at Parents' Place. These little people have now graduated from mama's arms to well-carpeted floors, and they lurch about babbling on play telephones, climb in little plastic chairs, and occasionally hit each other with whatever is at hand. Because I had attended the very first meeting when Ian was newborn, I was thrilled to go again and see how all these little persons have grown and developed. It was on our way there that I experienced the perk.

We were wending our way through several tree-canopied streets when I saw it: a road sign that read CAUTION BUTTERFLY ZONE. I was utterly charmed but totally mystified.

"Beth, did you see that butterfly sign? What on earth does it mean? Is it for real? Why does one need to be cautious about butterflies? Are they hostile?"

She explained to me that Pacific Grove is one of the few migratory destinations in the world for the Monarch butterfly and that the area in which we were riding was one of their specific destinations.

"But why does that fact warrant a sign asking motorists to be cautious?"

"Mom, from October 1 until the end of November there can be literally thousands of butterflies swarming across the road on their way to the various groves of trees where they spend the winter. You could injure or even kill them."

Well, that image put me in a deep "think" that lasted at least twenty minutes. I was touched by the tender seriousness of this city's residents in preserving the well-being of these delicate and gorgeous creatures. In addition to being touched, I was sufficiently intrigued to later call the Pacific Grove Chamber of Commerce and learn more about their provision for the Monarchs.

I was told that there is a city ordinance which mandates punishment by a heavy fine for anyone caught hurting or interfering in any way with the safety of the butterflies. Also, each year on the second Saturday of October, every preschool and kindergarten child in town dresses up as a Monarch butterfly, and the whole city welcomes the returning Monarchs with a six-block parade. I asked my informant how many butterflies make their sometimes 1800-mile trek to Pacific Grove. She happily reported that thus far there were about ten thousand, but more would be coming. She concluded by pronouncing: "These butterflies are a very big deal to us." That statement and my recently acquired knowledge made my insides smile and go soft.

Creation is filled with stunning variety and exquisite beauty. The delicate, intricate, and fragile as well as the strong, mighty, and powerful testify sweetly to the richness of the Creator. It is crucial that we attend not only to the needs of the human beings that inhabit this earth, but also to the preservation of the countless creatures that contribute to the beauty and balance of our God-given environment. I need to be reminded that "in wisdom" he made them all, and a part of my reverencing him is my reverencing all the earth's creatures: humans, animals, flowers, trees, and yes, the ten thousand butterflies hidden in those trees.

"Oh Father, the God of all creation, enable me to revel in the works of your hands with a renewed vision and a protective enthusiasm. The earth is indeed 'full of your creatures.' In reverencing you, I also must reverence them. Amen."

JOY BEADS

Barbara Johnson

Now to him who is able to do
immeasurably more than all we ask or
imagine, according to his power
that is at work within us.

EPHESIANS 3:20

When I bought some new makeup recently, the salesgirl told me that if I dropped a little BB in the bottle and shook it before each use, the makeup wouldn't get thick and gooey. Not having BBs on hand at home, I called my son Barney because he has guns and supplies.

"Why in the world would you want a BB, Mom?" he asked.

Rather than go into a long explanation, I just said "Never mind" and figured I could look elsewhere. Then I told my husband I needed a BB, knowing he'd probably ask for an explanation, too. Sure enough. This time I gave him one and wondered if it was worth it.

A day or so later, Bill came in smiling broadly and looking like he had something wonderful to show me. What he had was a huge plastic carton. Inside were 10,000 — that's ten thousand! — BBs.

"BBs only come in tens of thousands," he told me proudly. I smiled appreciatively and took *one*.

Recently I saw that plastic carton full of 9,999 BBs lying on a shelf in our garage. I got to thinking how much it's like the riches of God in Christ Jesus. We have *more* than enough. Much, much more than we'll ever be able to use: forgiveness, grace, mercy, love . . . We have abundant resources just waiting for us to use! God's riches are beyond anything we could ask or even dare to imagine! If my life gets gooey and stale, I have no excuse.

As a child, my Sunday-school teacher always told me, *"God's blessing bucket is bottomless."* Her favorite Bible story was about the widow of Zarephath. When you live in obedience to God, she would tell us, the jar of oil never runs dry; the bowl of flour never becomes empty. I never knew what the oil and the flour meant, and I guess I didn't give it a second thought at the time.

Now I know about the oil of anointing to fulfill our work for God and the grain it takes to do that. God has never withheld resources from me, although I've gone through loss after loss. It takes just one BB to shake things up: the decision to be joyful. Life can't get thick and unmanageable if you drop joy beads in the jar. It puts worries in their place: you see how senseless it is to use today to clutter up tomorrow's opportunities with problems left over from yesterday.

We can learn something from the story of a Spanish adventurer who trekked across the deserts of Egypt in search of treasure. After years of wandering, he found a note buried in the sand at the foot of the pyramids: *The treasure is buried in a shepherd's field in Spain.* The adventurer studied the map lying with the note and realized after all his searching that the treasure was buried in his own backyard!

What is the treasure we have in earthly vessels, right here, right now? It is Jesus Christ, our Redeemer, and the precious Holy Spirit. It is the capacity to be divinely happy wherever we are, in whatever circumstances. Talk about a perk!

God has given us good measure, pressed down, shaken together, and running over. But most of the time, we need only one BB.

"Dear Lord Jesus, make me aware of your precious treasure that is all around me. Your Word says you have given me more than enough. I celebrate my heritage as your child. Amen."

GUIDANCE OUT OF NOWHERE

Luci Swindoll

When I am afraid, I will trust in you.

PSALM 56:3

A very dear friend of mine who teaches elementary school music got a timely reminder recently of how much simpler life can be when God is in the picture. One Monday afternoon she was feeling apprehensive about having to change the date for a musical program on the school calendar. It meant she had to face the principal, ask for the change, and possibly have her request rejected. As you may know, one can't just arbitrarily switch the dates of the orchestra concert and the big basketball game, for example. These events are determined months in advance and are generally set in concrete!

As she busied herself in her classroom, she rehearsed what she would say to the principal. The fear began to rise in her so much that her anxiety was out of proportion to her upcoming request. She had that "fretful" feeling.

While dusting off her desk, she swept a small scrap of paper to the floor. When she picked it up, she was amazed to read the words, "When I am afraid, I will trust in you." She could hardly believe her eyes; it was just the encouragement she needed to accomplish the task at hand.

She smiled to herself, took a deep breath, and walked straight to the principal's office for her talk. Everything worked out beautifully, and the date was changed on the calendar with only minor adjustments.

Several days later, a little girl in one of her music classes came up to her and whispered, "Mrs. Jacobs, have you by any chance seen a piece of paper with the words, 'When I am afraid, I will trust in you' written on it?" My friend told the child she had seen that paper and it was at her desk.

"Is it yours, Rachel?" The child told her it was. Wanting to make the most of the moment, my friend asked, "Are you all right, honey? How did you happen to have that piece of paper in the first place? Is there anything I can help you with?"

Rachel confided, "Well, remember a few

days ago when we had to take all those tests? I was afraid I couldn't pass, so my mom put that note in my lunch box that day, and it really helped me. Then somehow I lost it."

My friend then explained how the child's loss was her gain. She expressed that she too had feared something, found the paper on the floor, and was reminded to face and overcome that fear by trusting God. The very thing that had calmed the heart of the little child was the same thing that calmed the heart of the wise and mature schoolteacher.

Fear is indiscriminate. It affects all of us regardless of our age or position in life. Whether our fear is absolutely realistic or out of proportion in our minds, our greatest refuge is Jesus Christ.

You may wonder how to find that refuge. It is really very simple: as you walk through your days, you encounter various situations in life that trouble you. If you're like me there are decisions that must be made that seem bigger than I have the capacity to handle. Or there's a relationship in my life that's out of whack and needs attention. Perhaps it's a money problem or a doctor's dreaded report that has me upset.

At times like these we can either quiver in our boots and become paralyzed by that "deer caught in the headlights" phenomenon, we can retreat completely convincing ourselves that the problem doesn't exist, or we can talk to the One who is able to calm our apprehensions and fears and give us courage to move ahead with a heart of confidence and assurance. In other words, we can pray.

There are times you might be so fearful that all you can say is, "Lord, I'm scared. Please give me peace because I'm placing my trust in you. I know you can meet me right here. Please do!" And he will. He will enter into your mind and calm you with his presence.

God wants us to know that he is with us; he is for us. That's why he has given us this verse. Write it out on a piece of paper today and tuck it in your purse as a reminder that he is greater than your fear.

"What a blessing it is, Lord, to know you are my strength and my confidence. I am so glad I don't have to depend on myself at this moment. Give me the comfort I need from you to meet my fear head-on, knowing full well that I am completely safe when I put my trust in you. Amen."

HAVE YOU CHECKED YOUR WARDROBE LATELY?

Barbara Johnson

Therefore, as the elect of God,
holy and beloved, put on
tender mercies, kindness, humility,
meekness, long-suffering,
bearing with one another,
and forgiving one another . . .
but above all these things
put on love.

COLOSSIANS 3:12–14 (nkjv)

Like everybody else, I have to get up and get dressed every day. Too often I go to my closet and throw my hands in the air: "I don't have anything to wear!" My husband, Bill, shakes his head and laughs. "No really," I whine, peering into my closet and surveying the rod of hangers drooping with weight.

"This jacket is too worn," I say to myself. "It's got little fuzz balls all over it. This dress has gotten too small. That blouse hangs wrong at the shoulders; why did I let my sister talk me into buying it? This little number is totally outdated; I can't wear that. The blue sweater is the wrong color for my skin, and the pink one has a stain. Here's a good blouse, but I always feel frumpy in it. This one's uncomfortable; it chafes. This skirt is too long. This one's too short . . ."

I sit on the edge of my bed and pout: "Nothing to wear!" Bill is already back in the kitchen, oblivious to my dismay.

Seasons come and go. Clothing styles change. Different regions of my anatomy fluctuate in size. Fabrics wear thin, fade, and lose their appeal. Good thing I have another closet with unlimited choices. I have a wardrobe that will never fade, wear out, or go out of style. Best of all, these clothes fit perfectly each time I pull them out and put them on.

Have you checked your spiritual wardrobe lately? The apostle Paul listed the garments of the Holy Spirit in his letter to Colossian believers. First on his list is *tender mercies*. Also known as compassion, tender mercies are acts of empathy for weak or

47

hurting people. They are usually motivated by feeling the same kind of pain as others or being able to imagine it. I call tender mercies the underwear of God's wardrobe — personal and next-to-the-skin. They are the foundation for everything that goes on the outside.

Next on Paul's list is *kindness*. Everyone can use a warm-hearted deed as simple as a smile. But kindness is more than that. It's an attitude that becomes part of your life-style. It involves treating others with honor and significance. The attitude of kindness is everyday stuff like a great pair of sneakers. Not frilly. Not fancy. Just plain and comfortable.

Humility is next. No matter how much we win or lose in life, God wraps us in a beautiful cloak of grace. When we're humiliated, he loves us exactly as we are. When we're in the limelight, we understand the big part he played in our success.

Meekness is one of my favorite things to wear. Some people think it's nondescript, but I disagree. Meekness makes it possible to endure difficult circumstances and poor treatment at the hands of others. It is a durable garment with interesting textures. And meekness looks different on everyone!

How about *long-suffering?* Sometimes I wish that old rag would just wear out so I could get something more glamorous and colorful. But I know God has fashioned even this to enhance my life. There are times when long-suffering is the only appropriate thing to wear for a particular occasion — and then I'm glad it's in the closet.

Bearing with others and *forgiveness* are the outerwear of God's designs. They are the last things we pull on over everything else before we go out into the world. It would get awfully cold without them. They protect us from the elements and keep the wind from blowing down our necks. As we go in and out of various experiences, we button them up often and keep trudging.

Above all else, Paul says, put on *love.* Without this, we are never fully dressed. You might think of love as your best hat or the jeweled pin on the lapel of life. It is that one essential accessory you should never leave behind. Dust it off, shine it up. Never go out without it!

Put away the shabby clothing of the past and enjoy all the garments in your spiritual wardrobe. Dress like the woman God made you to be. He replaces sackcloth and ashes for garments of praise!

♥

"Dear God, thank you for the garments of grace you've prepared for me. I like your style. When I'm feeling poor and ragged, I'll remember you keep your children well-dressed. Amen."

SONGS OF THE HEART

Patsy Clairmont

The LORD God is my strength,
and he has made my feet
like hinds' feet, and makes me
walk on my high places.

HABAKKUK 3:19 (nasb)

Have you noticed that we tend to be thematic people? And that other people's themes are easier to identify than our own? Throughout the years, I've had several consistent life themes that have slid in and out of my repertoire.

When I was an agoraphobic, my theme song sounded more like a dirge. "I can't," "It's too difficult," and "I'm afraid" were just a few of the phrases in my discordant refrain. Every day and every task seemed overwhelming. I gave up on a lot of life and gave in to fear as my scary companion. People tried to help me find a more melodic song to sing, but my mournful minuet with fear continued like a long-playing record.

In time people's tolerance waned. Avoiding me became easier than listening to my nerve-wracking recital. I guess they just needed a break. Eventually, even I tired of hearing my own broken-record whine.

That sad season in my life reminds me of a record my older brother Don used to enjoy when we were young: "The Little White Cloud that Cried" by Johnnie Ray. Don played it repeatedly day after day, week after week. C'mon, folks, how many times can one listen to a crying cumulus? I'm sure that's how people felt about me.

Gradually I moved into a different tempo, one that was more upbeat. I noticed that people didn't make such wide circles to skirt around me. Some were even drawn into my circle by the new song they were hearing. I guess "Singin' in the Rain" was easier to listen to than my former melancholy rendition of "Stormy Weather."

Ruth the Moabitess didn't sing in the rain, but she must have sung amidst the grain for her delightful spirit was immediately noticed by Boaz. I can almost hear Boaz humming "Ain't She Sweet," soon followed by a rousing duet of "Happy Days Are Here Again."

Ruth's journey to the grain fields had

been an arduous one. After being left a young childless widow, she moved to a far-away land to serve her grieving mother-in-law, Naomi. Ruth suffered the loss of her husband, her home, her family members, and her culture. That is a lot of loss. She certainly deserved a break. Who would have blamed Ruth if her theme song had become "Born to Lose"? Instead, we hear her heart sing, "I Will Follow You."

"I Will Follow You" was also Habakkuk's song. Well, he eventually sang that joyous melody. We don't know a lot about Habakkuk, but we do know he began where most of us do — with the well-worn words every disillusioned mind has sung: "Why me?" "Why this?" "Why now?" When he stopped complaining, took a break, and began to praise, Habakkuk wrote one of the most beautiful prayers ever set to music. Listen to a few of the lines and feel free to tap your toe and shout your praise: "Though the fig tree should not blossom, and there be no fruit on the vines, though the yield of the olive should fail, and the fields produce no food, though the flock should be cut off from the fold, and there be no cattle in the stalls, yet I will exult in the Lord, I will rejoice in the God of my salva-tion. The Lord God is my strength, and he has made my feet like hinds' feet, and makes me walk on my high places" (3:17–19 NASB).

This prayer-song, which never fails to move me, exposes the heart of a man who went from rags to riches spiritually. Habakkuk discovered that, even if his crops and flocks failed, he would still have reason to rejoice. I've been there, too. I fretted in lean years about our crops (groceries) and our flock (family). And I, too, discovered that "His Name Is Wonderful," regardless of stormy seasons and slim pickins.

Do you have a theme song that others hear when they listen to your life? What title would you give it? Would your family agree?

"Dear Lord Jesus, some of us need to sing a new song. Will you teach us the words? Help us to sing in harmony with the Holy Spirit so our song will delight your heart. Amen."

GET OUT OF THAT RUT

Embracing the Risky and Wild

Go For It!

Marilyn Meberg

So then, banish anxiety from your heart
and cast off the troubles of your body.

ECCLESIASTES 11:10

There's a certain love of the risky and wild in
me that rarely needs encouragement. One of
those more delicious fulfillments of my wild
side occurred years ago when I was teaching
English at Biola University.

On a Saturday afternoon preceding the
beginning of winter semester, Beth and I
drove over to the school so I could put my
class syllabuses on the secretary's desk for
typing and distribution to classes on Monday morning. I needed to get into my office,
but the building was locked. That meant I
had to walk all the way over to the administration building and pick up a master key.

I grumbled and snorted my way over
there, asked for a key to the building, was
told I had to leave my driver's license,

agreed to those peculiar terms, made my way back to my office, left the syllabuses, and was irritated that I had to walk all the way back to the administration building to return the key.

At the time of this story, I was driving a little blue Fiat convertible that I adored. I experienced an indescribable sense of euphoria whizzing freely about in that little convertible. Because of its size I was able to zip in and out of spaces prohibited to the larger, more traditional, and sedate cars. One of my delights was to experience just how many places I could go that bigger cars could not.

Looking fondly now at my little car in the Biola parking lot where Beth was waiting patiently for me, I got one of those deliciously wild and risky ideas. The Biola buildings are connected by a network of sidewalks that crisscross all over campus. As I walked those various sidewalks during a typical class day, I often mused about the width of the walks and whether my Fiat would fit on them. *What a fabulous time to find out*, I thought.

Leaping into the car, I announced to Beth that we were in a hurry and then pulled onto the sidewalk leading to the administration building. We were a perfect fit: on either side of the tires was only an inch or two of sidewalk to spare. With an exuberant whoop I exclaimed, "Beth, look at what a tidy fit we are . . . don't you love this?" She shot me a look of withering disapproval that only a sixteen-year-old can muster and chided, "Mom, you are not for real!"

Undaunted, I buzzed forward. But my euphoria was short-lived as I heard a jarringly loud honk behind me. To my amazement there was a big fat Biola security car poised by the sidewalk entrance; the driver was motioning me to return to the parking lot. I was stunned. Where on earth had he come from?

Well, this is a bit sticky, I mused to myself. *Here I am, a faculty member, jauntily driving on the sidewalk knowing full well I should not be. What do I do? I'm where I'm not supposed to be doing what I'm not supposed to be doing . . . it can't get any worse. So why stop?*

My pertinacity inspired the security guy to turn on his siren and red lights and to pull onto the sidewalk in hot pursuit. I noticed in my side mirror that his tires hung over both sides of the sidewalk leaving unsightly tread marks in the grass. *He should be ashamed of himself,* I thought. I also thought I'd better stop.

When he asked where I was going, I told

him I was heading over to the administration building to pick up my driver's license. That didn't sit well with him. When he asked why I was on the sidewalk, I told him I was in mid-life crisis and that sometimes I got irresistible urges. He wasn't responsive to that either.

I told this story not long afterward to a gathering of women, and one of them sent me a bumper sticker that read: "If you don't like the way I drive, get off the sidewalk!"

This brand of risky living may not be to your taste, but let me encourage you to stretch to the degree that feels safe to you. It may be no more wild than eating dessert before dinner. You might graduate to something like wearing your wedding dress to the grocery store. Whatever it is, consider the degree of risky and wild you can tolerate, and then go for it!

"Lord, teach us to 'banish anxiety from our hearts and cast off the troubles of our bodies.' Thank you for the assurance of your love for us which releases us to live out joyful impulses. Create within us a lightness of being that comes from knowing you. Amen."

RISKY LIVING

Patsy Clairmont

(Peter) cried out, "Lord, save me!"
Immediately Jesus reached
out his hand and caught him.

MATTHEW 14:30–31

My husband led a high-risk childhood. He
was wild and a risk-taker: you know, the type
you pray doesn't move in next door. He was
raised in Gay, Michigan (no, I didn't make
that up). Les, his four brothers, and sister,
Diane, lived in their small town (population
one hundred) nine hundred yards from Lake
Superior. In the winter they averaged two
hundred inches of snow — although it wasn't
unusual to have three and even four hundred
inches in one season. We can only imagine
the snow adventures that created.

One winter when Les was about ten years
old, he and some friends were breaking
snowdrifts off cliffs. They would walk out as
close to the cliff's edge as they dared and

then kick until the drift would break off and tumble to the ground twenty-five feet below. Once Les misjudged the edge and tumbled headlong to the ground below. The large accumulation of snow softened his landing, but the broken snowdrift followed Les. In seconds the only sign of him was two feet sticking out, and they were kicking. His friends scrambled to his rescue, digging him out with their hands.

Now that's enough to leave a permanent set of chill bumps on a kid and on his mother (if she ever found out). Some risks aren't worth taking. Like bear tampering . . .

One of Les's childhood diversions was to throw rocks at bears while they were dining at the dump. (Call me cautious, but I wouldn't have the starch to throw a rock at a bear if it was stuffed and mounted, much less if it was breathing.) When the bears became agitated, they would chase the kids up a hill until the children were out of sight. Believing they were rid of their tormentors, the bears would return to the dump only to have these daring imps reappear.

One time Les was visiting his cousins, and they decided to stir up some bear fur — only these annoyed bears became ticked. The boys ran until their hearts were in their mouths and still the bears were in hot pursuit. All parties involved were thinking about the fellows becoming the third course of a seventeen-course meal. But of course, since I'm married to Les, you can guess that he narrowly escaped, as did his cousins.

Les did decide that, after his brush with Smokey and the bandits, he wouldn't bug any more bears. Some risks aren't worth taking.

My friend Connie told me that when her husband of many years decided he wanted to be a free agent and play the field, she was devastated. She had just purchased a business, and with it came considerable financial responsibility. Reeling from the divorce and feeling financially overwhelmed, she was taken even further aback by an additional business offer. She was given an opportunity to become a partner in a building. Normally guarded, Connie was not one to wade beyond the safety of the shore. But with knees knocking and realizing she was at risk of losing every cent she had for her future, Connie took the plunge. She confessed it was the scariest thing she had ever done.

That was four years ago. Today she not only has a thriving business but also the building she invested in is one of the loveliest in our town. Connie learned that some risks are worth taking.

That's the problem with risks: some are worth taking, some aren't. Some of the risks I've taken that turned out poorly have been the greatest teachers for making good future choices. And some sure-shot risks have been long-term detrimental. Hmm, this is complex. Bad could be good, good could be miserable, bad could be disabling, and good could turn out great. I guess that's why it's called a risk.

I'm really not one to dive headlong into life, but I don't want to miss the wave and be left high and dry on the shore. I wonder if that's how Peter felt when he stepped from the boat's safety to join Jesus in the raging sea (Matthew 14:28–32). Peter wanted to take the risk, but then he focused on the storm and began to sink. Stepping on the water wasn't risky for Peter because he was walking toward Jesus. No, the big risk was taking his eyes off the Lord and being overwhelmed by his circumstances. Even then the Lord extended a helping hand.

That's the safety factor in facing life's risks: Jesus. If you are walking toward him to the best of your ability, he will see you through life's unpredictable waters — but you must risk launching the boat. Just ask Peter or Connie.

"Lord, what a risk you took loving us. Give us the wisdom and courage to risk loving you in return. Amen."

It's Later
Than You Think

Luci Swindoll

What I mean . . . is that the
time is short. For this world in its
present form is passing away.

1 CORINTHIANS 7:29, 31

Funny thing about *time:* Every one of us
knows we have only twenty-four hours a day,
yet we try our best to think of ways to make
each day last longer or become shorter to suit
our preferences. While the clock ticks out the
same number of minutes at the same rate
every day, we try to *save* them like pennies in
a jar, so we can spend them someday somewhere else, whenever we choose.

Not a bad idea, but it just doesn't work
that way. Many of us cannot grasp the truth
that the time allotted to us on this earth is
sufficient for all the Lord has planned for us
to do. We don't need one minute more or

one minute less to get the job done: the job of *living*.

When I was a child, our family had a chiming clock that had been handed down through the generations and was a well-loved treasure. On the hour, of course, it would chime out the time, and by it we kept on schedule with meals and departures and awakening and bedtime. Many nights, from our respective bedrooms, each of us would call out the number of chimes until the last one stopped.

One night, after we had all gone to bed about midnight, the clock began to gong and we started our audible ritual: "Nine . . . ten . . . eleven . . . twelve." Just as we closed our mouths after shouting out TWELVE! the clock struck thirteen. We could hardly believe our ears. *Where did that come from?* I wondered, as we all laughed heartily from our beds. Then, almost in perfect unison, we called out: "It's later than you think!"

For most of us, that's the problem: our greatest fear is running out of time. So we hurry through life trying desperately to get everything done: working overtime, eating fast food in the car, racing down the freeway. We've gone from *The One Minute Manager* to *The One Minute Mother* to *One Minute Wisdom*. Life itself encourages us to hurry. I can do my laundry twice as fast as my grandmother did; I can travel coast to coast faster than my father ever could; I can handle correspondence that took my mother hours with a few keystrokes and mouse clicks. And yet, I seem to have less time than they did. *What has happened?*

In our quest to save time, we're losing something. I thought the other day about how my grandparents valued time. They always had time for my parents and my brothers and me; they had time for music in their home (each of them was a competent musician); they emphasized beautifully served meals, family reunions, and long conversations. It seemed they had time for everything in life that was important, because *they took time to live.* They treasured the biblical injunction that proclaims, "This is the day the Lord has made; let us rejoice and be glad in it" (Psalm 118:24).

Today, this very day, why don't you think of something that takes a bit of extra time to do and *do it.* Do it for yourself. Do it for a family member. Do it for a neighbor or friend. Do it for the Lord. Maybe it will be an act of generosity or a moment of kindness directed toward a loved one or a stranger. Perhaps it will be simply singing a hymn of praise and thanksgiving because your heart is so full of gratitude.

Don't wait for another time. Rejoice in *this* day and be glad! Tonight, your clock *could* strike thirteen.

"Father, give me the grace today to take time. Time to be with you. Time to be with others. Time to enjoy the life you have given me. Help me remember that today is the day you have made. May I rejoice and be glad in it! Amen."

GOLDEN MOMENTS

Barbara Johnson

"Be strong and do not give up,
for your work will be rewarded."

2 CHRONICLES 15:7

One day I made a list of things I had to do,
knowing I was so bewildered and confused
by pain that I might forget. I wrote:

1. Get up.
2. Survive.
3. Go to bed.

Some days, that's more work than you'll
do the rest of your life. Some days, your
work is to be patient with yourself. Other
days, your work is just to be yourself.

Recently I met an incredible lady who was
so good at the being-patient part. She
worked at a large publishing house that produced a huge number of Bibles — all kinds of
Bibles in all translations, sizes, and models.

We were shown how the Bibles are assembled, printed, and prepared for packaging and shipment. But one particular step in the process astounded me. You know how we take it for granted that Bibles have those little gold tabs denoting the various books? We came to one station where a woman was sitting on a stool with a pair of tweezers. She was picking up one small gold tab at a time and attaching it to the thin page of the Bible where it belonged.

The amazing thing is that this woman had been doing this for ten years! Over and over again, eight hours a day, four weeks a month, twelve months a year she had been picking up a little gold tab with tweezers and sticking it to a page of a Bible. I thought to myself, *I would last about one Bible doing this, for sure.* And yet I knew that life is made up of routine, and I started thinking about what those things were in my own life: brushing my teeth, making the bed, hanging up my clothes . . .

That day I decided that I wanted to do something to add meaning to all the boring routines in my day. I decided to celebrate them, to make them stand out as worthwhile accomplishments. I started by making a list of the things I do every single day without fail, including weekends. The list started with waking up to the same old alarm buzzer in the morning. It ended with switching off the lamp beside my bed in the evening.

My celebrations began when I traded in my buzzing clock for a radio alarm set to soft music. That was by far the biggest change I made. In other things, I made attitude adjustments. Glancing in the mirror on the way to the bathroom, I started smiling at myself. This started an amazing transformation from the inside out. As I brushed my teeth, I started praising God that I had teeth to brush. Making the bed became a ritual of prayer for my grandchildren. And so on . . .

Each time I faced a tedious, mundane task, I imbued it with enthusiasm. I tried to think up a personally edifying reason for doing what I was doing. I made sure no mundane or trivial task was overlooked. I wanted to fill each one with a sense of being golden, like the stickers placed with care on the pages of those Bibles.

With practice in patience, all my moments are becoming golden. These moments include filling the cat's dish or wiping off countertops, things that take a few seconds or a few minutes. Ho-hum days begin to glow — just enough to make things look rosy. Busy, stressful days are lighter when I remember my resolution to be patient and steady.

Then on really bad days, I think about the patience of the lady sitting on the stool in the publishing house where Bibles are produced by the millions. I think about all the hands that will touch the pages of those Bibles and rely on those little golden tabs. And I believe my tedious moments will be redemptive, too.

"Oh Lord, because of your life in me, each moment of my life has value and potential for significance — if I will only celebrate it. Infuse my attitude with the fruit of your Spirit, patience. Amen."

SIGN ON THE DOTTED LINE

Patsy Clairmont

And since we have gifts that differ according to the grace given to us, let each exercise them accordingly.

ROMANS 12:6 (nasb)

Risky behavior at this juncture in my life is wearing lace on my flannels and adding a jigger of orange juice to my Maalox. Although recently . . .

I signed on the dotted line to take a watercolor class with my friend Carol. A truly radical move. I'm a wanna-be artist whereas Carol *is* an artist. Even when we were kids Carol carried an easel while I carried an eraser. Carol's scribbles looked like Monet's while my finest effort had a curious resemblance to scribbles.

Through the years Carol has continued to develop in her artistic endeavors while I have continued to yearn. I have found that to yearn and to learn are quite different. One takes much less effort and a lot less risk than the other.

One day Carol mentioned she wanted to take a watercolor class at a local art store. She was reluctant to sign up because she didn't want to attend alone. That was when I heard myself say, "I'll take the class with you." (This wasn't one of those out-of-body experiences; it was an out-of-my-mind response.) "You will?" she said incredulously. "Yes," I answered, sounding as surprised as she looked.

During opening introductions in the first class, I knew I was in trouble. All the participants had prior art training . . . except me. (I decided the time I tripped over and spilled a can of paint on the porch probably wouldn't count.)

After the introductions, we moved into the opening exercises, which were designed to free us up and show us how watercolors moved and mixed. While the other students giggled and delighted in their lovely results, I had become bonded to my brush. I couldn't seem to cast my brush lavishly across the paper like the others. Instead, I made microscopic movements, as if the sable brush were cemented to my hand.

How one could be intimidated by a brush, a piece of paper, and some colors is beyond me, but I obviously was. The teacher kept taking my hand and forcing it across the paper in an attempt to limber me up. But as soon as she let go, I regressed to quarter-inch strokes. At the close of class she announced that the group was to do some artsy homework while I, who had to have the brush pried from my curled fingers, was told to practice moving my brush back and forth across an empty sheet of paper.

See Patsy. See Patsy's brush. See Patsy choke her brush.

The following week continued to be painful. I was the only one who didn't seem to grasp what we were doing. Duh. I thought about quitting, but I hate defeat (almost as much as humiliation). We tried different experiments with the wet paint such as sprinkling salt into it. This caused the paint to create soft shooting flares of color, adding a lovely dimension to the pictures. Well, actually mine looked more like . . . well . . . like globs of salt sitting in wet paint. I just didn't seem to have the gift.

Week after challenging week I wanted to quit but then told myself I was probably on the brink of Monetism. So I hung in there. I made it through the final class but no breakthrough broke through my lackluster performance. My pictures were a sight; some were a blur and a couple resembled images of birds, but we weren't sure if they were living or deceased.

Then it happened. I decided in the privacy of my home to attempt to put into practice some of the insights the teacher had shared. Before my eyes some flowers began to emerge, and it almost frightened me. I wasn't used to identifiable results; it was rather jolting.

Later that day Carol dropped by, and I cautiously slipped out my painting for her perusal. She remained speechless for some time. Then, regaining her voice, she whispered, "Patsy, this is good."

I knew it, I knew it. I would soon be on tour showing my pictures throughout the land. No, make that the world. Well, as soon as that nauseous wave of fame passed, reality settled in. Carol and I decided we should frame my flowers fast lest they wilt, and I lose my only proof of being an artist.

Carol and I concluded there are two types of artists. There are those who are artists by gift and those who are artists by guts. We know which one I am.

Now, how about you? Are you willing to take a risk (even if you're not the best in the field) and learn (not yearn for) a new skill, set a new goal, or help a dream come true? If so, please sign on the dotted line.

"Thank you, Lord Creator, that because of who you are, we can be more than we ever imagined. Amen."

PUT ANOTHER LOG ON THE FIRE

Marilyn Meberg

My people will live in peaceful
dwelling places, in secure homes,
in undisturbed places of rest.

ISAIAH 32:18

In spite of my oft-spoken philosophy of freedom to enjoy the moment, take a risk, or get out of a rut, I'm amazed at my own "rut-think" that periodically takes over. For instance, this past weekend I spoke at a pre-Christmas conference at Forest Home Christian Conference Center. I adore Forest Home and have been honored to fill a guest speaker spot for them many times through the years.

As I entered my little cabin, "The Biltmore," to put my stuff away and gather my thoughts, I noticed a most compelling arrangement of firewood all set up in the gorgeous stone fireplace. It appeared to need nothing more than a match. There was a bone-chilling cold in the air, but it was really too late to start a fire.

The next day, having spoken twice in the morning, I came back to my little Biltmore for a few delicious hours to myself. Looking again at that carefully laid arrangement of wood, I thought how much I would love doing a little writing, resting, and thinking utterly blank thoughts with a fire crackling in the background. But as I examined the wood more closely, I could see no way to start a fire. There was no paper, no kindling, no evidence whatsoever that a fire could start short of rubbing two sticks together. I thought, *Oh well, Marilyn, you don't need a fire. The cabin is warm . . . you're very comfortable as you are. Give up the idea.*

I hearkened back to the days of my youth when we sat around our stone fireplace in Amboy, Washington. There were two especially severe storms one winter that knocked out our electricity so that the fireplace was our only source of heat and our only source of fuel for cooking. I don't remember anything of the obvious inconvenience; I only remember feeling that I was a pioneer, braving the elements with courage and fortitude. (Of course, my courage and fortitude were totally dependent upon that of my parents — a fact that never occurred to me then.)

Overwhelmed with nostalgia, I determined I simply must have a fire in the fireplace! But how? I had noticed a tidy pile of wood on the little enclosed porch, so I poked around out there for a possible clue as to how to start my longed-for fire. Then it appeared! A two-gallon jug with the barely legible word "diesel" felt-penned on the side sat slightly behind the woodpile. So this is what one uses to start a fire! But wait a minute . . . how does one use diesel? It then seemed sensible to me that one simply needed to sprinkle, douse, or drench the wood with the diesel. I elected to drench the wood rather than sprinkle or douse.

As I was getting ready to touch the drenched wood with the lighter, I stopped abruptly and pondered, *What if this wood explodes into an uncontrollable inferno because I should have sprinkled rather than drenched? What if I destroy the entire conference center with but a flick of my lighter wand? I don't know anything about diesel except that it smells bad and cars that swallow it don't move fast. Well, hey . . . maybe a diesel fire won't move fast either . . . go for it, Marilyn!*

When the drenched wood and flame united in one beautiful moment of contained harmony, I was euphoric! All afternoon I sat in front of that crackling blaze, occasionally throwing another log on the fire and getting in touch with my nearly forgotten pioneer roots of courage and fortitude.

What if I had elected to douse my idea of a fire instead of dousing the wood with diesel? I would have never had that nearly three hours of soul-satisfying reverie. I nearly gave up the idea because I thought maybe I shouldn't risk it.

This may sound a bit naïve, but some of my greatest spiritual moments have been inspired by the unexpected and the simple. I can't tell you what a wonderful afternoon of Jesus-chat I experienced in front of my mildly risky fire. I truly felt as if I were in a God-given "peaceful dwelling place . . . in an undisturbed place of rest." All of that and a crackling fire, too.

"Dear God, I love the fact that wherever I am, you are there, too. You are with me in front of the fire as well as in church. You are with me in the night as well as in the morning. You are with me in times of sadness and in times of gladness. May I never be in such a rut that I limit this awareness of your creative presence. Amen."

FANCY FOOTWORK

Patsy Clairmont

"In the name of Jesus Christ
of Nazareth, walk."

ACTS 3:6

I hate being stuck, don't you? Like in traffic jams where, by the time the traffic clears, you have become executor of the estate for your newfound friends in the car next to you. Or stuck in a checkout lane because an item isn't marked and the teller has to wire Taiwan for a price check. How about the times you get stuck in a conversation with salespeople, an angry boss, or someone who just is a hopeless prattler. If that's not bad enough, have you ever been superglued to something? Now, honey, that's stuck. (My friend, in an attempt to do a fast repair on her earring, superglued her finger to her earlobe.)

Life is full of stuck possibilities. In fact, when you think about it, we are kind of stuck here on planet earth until further notice. Or, as my hymnal puts it, "Till the Roll Is Called Up Yonder." Makes me think we better make the best out of stuck lest life turn into one big rut.

I hate ruts. They're so . . . so rutlike. Ruts are common, unimaginative, and oh, so boring. I know because I've spent time in them. Actually, I even took up emotional residence in a couple. To make them comfortable (I planned on staying), I even decorated them. I adorned the walls with excuses: "I can't," "I tried," and "I don't wanna." Those were just a few of the plagues, I mean plaques, I hung in my ruts.

Instead of "Welcome," my doormat stated, "Enter at Your Own Risk." You see, rut-dwellers tend to be irksome and dreary. Besides, ruts are personal, and normally it's only one to a rut. The rut-ee, if crowded, could growl, and like a sleeping dog, it is best to let the person lie.

I can usually spot a rut-dweller from twenty paces (takes one to know one). They lack luster, imagination, energy, and interest. They tend to slurp, slump, and sleep a lot. They prefer to gripe rather than grow, and they enjoy whine with their candlelight.

Who really wants to be like that? I saw that hand! No, you don't. In your heart of hearts (does that mean we have two?), you know ruts offer no future. At least not one with sparkle, celebration, and verve. Let's rid our lives of ruts even if we have to excavate to find our way out.

Have you ever observed excavators? First thing they do is send out surveyors to assess. This is where the Holy Spirit and several of your wise friends (not other rut-dwellers) can assist. The Holy Spirit can reveal to you why you are stuck, and he can empower you to change (although he won't usually do all the work without your involvement). Your friends can help strengthen your resolve and pray for you in the process. Solomon informs us of the value of team participation: "Two are better than one . . . If one falls down [into a rut], his friend can help him up" (Ecclesiastes 4:9–10).

After the surveyors comes the heavy equipment to break up the hard stuff. Hmm, like our heads? Or perhaps our hearts. "And I shall take the heart of stone out of their flesh and give them a heart of flesh, that they may walk in My statutes and keep My ordinances, and do them" (Ezekiel 11:19–20 NASB).

To walk in his ways is our goal. His ways rescue us from our rut-dwelling ways. Because ruts have limited walking space, rut-dwellers are more into sitting, remote-ing, and molding rather than moving. Whereas when we walk in his ways, they are challenging, enlightening, and adventuresome.

My mom is eighty-one, and she's proud of it. In the past few years of her life she has become a walker. Every day she heads out for a hike. Sometimes it's just laps around her circular driveway, but she keeps those size-four feet a-movin'. Mom's determined no mold will grow in her socks. Recently she went to a podiatrist, and the doctor was impressed with how healthy her feet are. I'm sure a portion of her fancy footwork is due to all the walking she does.

Now just imagine what might happen if we were to step out of our old routine and deliberately walk in his ways. Why, we might even do a little break dancing on our way up and out of that hard place.

C'mon, sister rut-dwellers, boogie out of there. Risk life!

"Jesus, you lead; I want to follow. Amen."

UNEXPECTED DELIGHTS

Luci Swindoll

"For I am the LORD, your God,
who takes hold of your right hand
and says to you, Do not fear;
I will help you."

ISAIAH 41:13

On the morning of August 11, 1991, I went
to my friend Mary's home for breakfast. As
she was setting the table, I broke my left leg. I
don't usually do this sort of thing, but I was
having such a relaxing time puttering around
on her patio, watering and pruning a few
plants. In my effort to pull a loose branch off
a big fern (we are talkin' *really big* here, folks:
the fern that ate L.A.), my feet flew out from
under me and I hit the pavement with a splat.
I could swear I heard the bone break. You
don't want me to describe the sound.

Not knowing the extent of the injury, Mary
took me to the emergency room at a nearby
hospital where I was admitted, x-rayed, and

told I had a six-inch break in the fibula, just above the ankle. (That's the smaller of the two bones that runs between the knee and the foot.) I was offered the choice between having no surgery (but wearing a cast from toes to groin for eight to twelve months) or having a metal plate with six or seven screws surgically inserted in the break area, which would help me heal in only four months. I chose the latter option.

Well, what an interesting four months those were! First of all, my orthopedic surgeon, Dr. Michael Kropf, turned out to be young, good-looking, gentle, and tremendous fun. Even when he changed my initial cast by sawing it off with a vibrating blade and I got a look at my swollen, bruised leg for the first time, he was very tender. He even permitted me to include Mary, who at my request took pictures of the whole procedure. (She got a little queasy, but I did just fine.)

On the third day after the fall and my release from the hospital, I made a conscious decision about the coming months. I wasn't going to let my broken leg, my cast, or my crutches get in the way of my life. In fact, I wrote in my journal (and I quote), "I'm not going to let this stop me. I'll look at every day as a challenge and watch the Lord make the crooked places straight. He knows my need, and he'll meet me there." And did he ever!

There were numerous occasions during that time of healing when he delighted me with his faithfulness. In spite of my broken leg I went to work every day, to Colorado on vacation, and to Italy for Marilyn's daughter's wedding. I never missed a single speaking engagement in six different states.

The most wild experience, however, was in early December when I flew to Chicago where I was to change planes for the Twin Cities. It was very cold and snowing in Chicago when I was met at my gate by an American Airlines attendant with a wheelchair. When he wheeled me over to board my connecting flight, the word "canceled" was flashing on the screen. "Is this flight to Minneapolis/St. Paul *really* canceled?" I asked in all seriousness.

"Indeed it is, ma'am," he replied. "That airport is shut down, and nobody is flying in there today. Sorry."

I asked to be pushed over to a pay phone, where I called my hostess in Minneapolis to report what had happened. "Oh, Luci," she said, "I called you this morning to tell you not to come, but you had already left. I feel so bad that you made this trip for nothing."

Well, as it turned out, it wasn't for

"nothing" after all. When I explained my plight to the guy pushing my wheelchair, he smiled sweetly and asked, "May I take you to lunch? Then we'll get you on a return flight to California. Would that be okay?"

Later that evening, I invited a few friends over for pizza. As we were each discussing the events of our day, they asked sympathetically, "And what did you do today, Luci, being in a wheelchair and all?" I *delighted* in telling them I had flown to Chicago for lunch!

Each of us has something broken in our lives: a broken promise, a broken dream, a broken marriage, a broken heart . . . and we must decide how we're going to deal with our brokenness. We can wallow in self-pity or regret, accomplishing nothing and having no fun or joy in our circumstances; or we can determine with our will to take a few risks, get out of our comfort zone, and see what God will do to bring unexpected delight in our time of need.

Ernest Hemingway puts it this way in *A Farewell to Arms*: "The world breaks everyone and many are strong at the broken places." I challenge you to be one of the many. Take that step of faith and ask God to surprise you in a unique way that only he has the flair to accomplish.

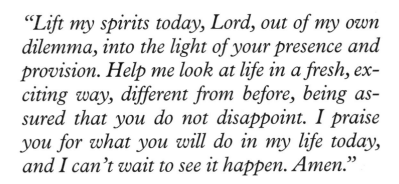

"Lift my spirits today, Lord, out of my own dilemma, into the light of your presence and provision. Help me look at life in a fresh, exciting way, different from before, being assured that you do not disappoint. I praise you for what you will do in my life today, and I can't wait to see it happen. Amen."

YAHOO!

Marilyn Meberg

For in Christ all the fullness
of the Deity lives in bodily form,
and you have been given fullness
in Christ, who is the head over
every power and authority.

COLOSSIANS 2:9–10

"Now do I assume, Pat, that you've signed up for these lessons to improve your skills in skating around the rink?"

"Well, sure, I need to improve in that, too, but that's not why I signed up for lessons."

Debbie, a figure-skating instructor who would still be skating professionally if a back injury had not interfered with her career, looked at Pat warmly and said, "Tell me what you hope to learn in your lessons."

"I want to skate faster, do spins, and maybe ultimately a double or triple axel."

Debbie sucked in her breath, quickly appraised Pat's fifty-eight-year-old body, and with an enthusiastic nod said, "Okay . . . let's get to work!"

I met Pat Wenger at Pepperdine University where we were both studying to complete our master's degree in counseling psychology. Like me, she had been a teacher and was embarking on a second career. Because of many personal similarities, we immediately became good friends. Ultimately we shared a suite of offices together when we went into private practice. Pat lives in the desert part time so when she's here we get together frequently. (She lives three condos up from Luci. Theirs is a troubled street, to say the least.) Pat's the one who enthusiastically sells my tapes at the Joyful Journey conferences.

Yielding to an inner itch, Pat bought ice skates a year ago and now skates every Monday morning at our local mall rink. This time is set aside for just those in the skating club; kids and others are not allowed. Pat had not been on ice skates since she was ten years old, but each time she glides the ice now, there's increased assurance and a growing desire to do what was denied her as a child. She wants to learn to figure skate: not just go around and around the rink but occasionally twirl and jump!

Though much of me lauds her wild and

risky aspirations, there's another part of me that feels nervous for her safety. With my typically generous spirit I asked her how she could sell my tapes if she became a quadriplegic from one too many spins. She told me she would stop short of that and just go for the paraplegic designation so she could at least point.

There is an undeniable glow that radiates from Pat for hours after she's been skating. Obviously something is released in her as she harmonizes her skates and body on that slippery ice. I've seen that same glow on the faces of a darling couple who are in their eighties and who also skate at the rink every Monday morning. I don't see them jumping and twirling, though. When I pointed that out to Pat her response was that when she reaches her eighties she won't twirl and jump anymore either.

I rather envy all this. I have never been on ice skates in my life and have no desire to start now. There is, however, a certain freedom and joy that comes from the mastery of something seemingly beyond our abilities. The idea of always playing it safe, never venturing out of our comfort zone, and refusing to broaden the borders of our experience is stultifying.

That being the case, I've decided to sign

up for line-dancing lessons. Don't call me on Tuesday nights because I'll be at the Lariat Club in Palm Springs. Yahoo!

"Because of you, Lord Jesus, I have the fullness, the richness, the joyfulness of your total Deity within my being. Because you have given me the gift of salvation through your death on the cross, I have been set free from the weight of sin. I can enter into new experiences with ease and gratitude, and give you praise for these earthly pleasures. Amen."

USE THE MOMENTUM

Barbara Johnson

"You will receive power when the Holy Spirit comes on you."

ACTS 1:8

When I learned to ride a bicycle, I did it badly — at least in comparison to other neighborhood kids. I had no sense of balance. I'd wobble and roll, wibble and rock. I ended up with scraped knees and shins. It seemed no matter how much I wanted to, I couldn't get the two-wheeler to stay upright. I thought I'd be the only kid in second grade who couldn't ride a bike.

Fortunately, a neighborhood friend offered to teach me how to ride. He seemed so confident. "It's simple," he said. "The problem is you haven't got enough momentum going to keep in balance. Once you get going fast enough long enough you won't have any trouble at all."

"Uh, I don't think so," I answered. "Fast

96

enough, long enough? I think I hear my mother calling me home." And I was outta there.

But the next day, my friend was back. "Come on," he said. "I'll teach you how to ride today." He placed my hand on the handlebars of my red bicycle, a color that matched my emotion: deep fear. Trembling, I put my feet on the pedals while he held the bike steady. As we started to move forward he said, "When I let go, keep pedaling! Don't be afraid of the momentum. Use it!"

Tromp, tromp, tromp. Faster. Faster. I could hear his feet pounding the pavement. He kept me upright, but we were going fast. He was huffing when he shoved the seat of my bike forward. I shot down the road like a miniature rocket. From far behind me he yelled, "Use the momentum!" In panic, I kept pedaling just like he told me to — and I've been pedaling ever since.

In the kingdom of God, there are days we think we'll never learn our lesson because circumstances are too overwhelming. We view difficult circumstances as threats, not opportunities. We think they are going to hurt (and they might). We want to grow up and do exciting things like the other kingdom kids, but we don't want to bloody our knees and shins in the process.

Then the Holy Spirit whispers, "Come on, I'll teach you. I'll show you how to use momentum to get where God wants you to go with your life." The Holy Spirit knows we have what it takes to keep upright once we're shoved ahead. Yes, there are lots of wobbles along the way and more than a few dangers. But with time we learn to assume control over those things — if we just keep pedaling.

Webster's says *momentum* is "a property of a moving body that determines the length of time required to bring it to rest when under the action of a constant force or moment. Impetus."

God's wonderful Holy Spirit is a constant force in our lives. "For in him we live and move and have our being" (Acts 17:28). It is his impetus or shove that determines the length of time before we are required to use our own pedal power. God assumes we will exercise our own spiritual muscles to keep the momentum going. (He also wants us to slow down occasionally and take a rest.)

Someone said, "Our glory is not in never falling, but in rising each time we fall." I believe the secret of success is to stay cool and calm on top and pedal like crazy underneath. When you do fall and skin your knees, get up again and start all over under the impetus of the Holy Spirit. Stay in the race. Find your pace, then shift into cruise gear. Use the momentum!

"Lord Jesus, you have created me with all I need to fulfill your calling in my life. In your name, I will keep in spiritual shape to claim the prize of this high calling, remembering the Holy Spirit runs beside me and holds me up when I am off balance. Amen."

I DARE YOU

Luci Swindoll

Do not boast about tomorrow,
for you do not know what a
day may bring forth.

PROVERBS 27:1

More often than not I wish I had taken a camera along to capture some of the zany antics of Marilyn and me. Then maybe people would believe they really happened. However, the story I am about to relate is one of those rare occasions that I will be forever grateful no camera was available to record.

I had been living in Southern California for about a year when I received a call from a former Mobil Oil supervisor in Dallas; he was going to be vacationing in my area and would like to take me to dinner. I was thrilled with the prospect. Bill was a man I had dated a few times in Texas, and I always enjoyed his company . . . not to mention his tall, handsome looks and stylish grooming.

He was great fun to be with and a gentleman.

During the afternoon of the day Bill and I were to go out, I was riding along in Marilyn's car on the way to my house after we picked up her daughter from school. When I mentioned my *big evening,* she asked what I was planning to wear. "Well, I don't know . . . I really haven't thought about it. What do you think?" She liked the pantsuit I had on and suggested I wear that, but we both noticed a little spot on the front of the jacket; it really needed cleaning before it could be worn again. Marilyn said, "Oh well, you'll find something else, I'm sure," and turned on my street to drop me off.

"Wait a minute, Mar," I said. "Take me to the cleaners. I want to wear *this,* and if I don't get it there right now I can't have one-hour service." She stopped the car, looked at me, and inquired, "What will you wear home, Luci? You don't *have* to wear that outfit tonight, you know."

"Oh yes, I do. Please . . . just drive me to the cleaners and I'll take this off in the car and go home in my underwear. You'll take it in for me, won't you, and protect me from being seen?"

Immediately, I began to undress — jacket, blouse, slacks — as Marilyn headed for the cleaners. I hunkered down in my panties and bra while sweet little eleven-year-old Beth just stared at me in horror from the backseat. "Don't worry, honey," I assured her, "your mother won't let me be seen in my underwear. It's all right."

When we got to the cleaners' parking lot, I offered a silent prayer of thanks when I saw there was no one else there. Marilyn took my clothes, opened the door, and *left it wide open* as she proceeded into the cleaners to request one-hour service on my behalf. I scrambled to hide behind my purse, a box of Kleenex, and the steering wheel as another car pulled in and Beth slithered to the floorboard for cover.

When Marilyn got back in the car I choked on a half-hysterical giggle. "Marilyn . . . *how could you* leave that door open? What if a church member had driven up, or somebody who craved my body? What would I have done?"

In mock innocence she said, "I left the door open? How careless of me."

All the way home we laughed ourselves silly: she, from an upright position behind the steering wheel; I, hunched over with my head in my purse; and Beth, muttering from the backseat floorboard, "I don't believe this . . . I just don't believe it."

From inside my house, Marilyn brought me an old beat-up housecoat that I wouldn't wear to dump the garbage, much less in front of my apartment. But what could I do? I threw the robe on and marched up my walkway like that housecoat was what I always wore to pick up Beth from school. Even now, in the recesses of my mind, I can still hear Marilyn's cackling laughter as she sped away, and see Beth's head through the back window, shaking from side to side in perpetual incredulity.

Is there a moral to this crazy story? I think there is — an important one. Some of us are so set in concrete, we can't remember when we last laughed. Or created anything to laugh *at*. Everything is terribly serious. Heavy. Solemn. I'm not saying there's no place for this kind of attitude . . . but *every minute of the day?* Where is the joy? Where is the zaniness?

I dare you to do something today that will make you giggle. Invent it yourself. Bend a little. Dare to embrace something a bit risky and wild. And don't put it off until tomorrow. How do you know tomorrow will ever get here?

♥

"Creator of joy, help me this very day to look around and find something to laugh about. Doesn't have to be big. Doesn't have to be unusual. Just some little thing to remind me you are a God of jubilation. Keep me from being a stick in the mud! Help me to have fun today, and not put it off until tomorrow. Amen."

GET A LIFE

Staying in Your Own Orbit

ENOUGH IS ENOUGH

Luci Swindoll

But godliness with contentment is great gain. For we brought nothing into the world, and we can take nothing out of it. But if we have food and clothing, we will be content with that.

1 TIMOTHY 6:6–8

A few years ago a friend was spending the weekend with me, and when we awakened on Saturday morning she asked, "What shall we do today? Where would it be fun to go? The mall? The movies? The museum?" I think she was pretty stunned when I suggested we stay home. "And do *what?*" she questioned. "What about the beach, or the mountains, or the desert? Shouldn't we go someplace? It's Saturday!" She could not imagine staying home on a day we had set aside for fun.

"Well," I said, "why don't we do something here and enjoy what we already have?"

"Oh," she muttered. But she really became intrigued with the idea as I explained how I feel that we sometimes go running around looking for and buying more things — things we might already have. Why don't we just stay home and enjoy them?

That's what my friend and I did that day . . . *and she loved it.* We worked a jigsaw puzzle, listened to our favorite music, read to each other, played a game, made little meals, all the while having wonderful conversation. We went to bed that night completely satisfied.

Since that day, my friend has said to me many times, "That helped me so much. I've really learned to stay home and enjoy what I already have." Now when she comes here she never wants to leave. If we go to the mall or the movies, it's because I drag her. Not long ago I found a delightful little devotional book and I couldn't wait to buy it for her. The title? *Staying Home.*

What we learned that day is that enough is enough, even though there are times we're afraid to test it. We're kind of scared that what we have won't be enough to satisfy us.

One day I decided to count all the projects I had in my house (things I could make with my hands), and determine just how long I could go without buying another thing. These might be kits or models, or patterns for designs to be created out of paper, yarn, wood, or clay. When I finished counting, I figured I had *seven years'* worth of projects. I don't even know if I'll live that long!

Why do we so often feel that "there's something better out there"? I believe we're often uncomfortable with ourselves, so we go outside ourselves in search of someone, or something, or some place that will bring us contentment. We want to be somebody else, somewhere else, doing something else, and truthfully, we will settle for almost anything. And what does the Bible say about that? In Philippians 4:11, Paul says it all: "I have learned to be content whatever the circumstances."

If you struggle with contentment (and we all do sometimes), let me make three simple suggestions that might help:

1. Look around and consider your blessings. Read this morning's newspaper and be grateful for what didn't happen to you. Think about what you do have in a new light. As a single friend of mine says, "I'd rather want what I don't have than have what I don't want."

2. Look around and consider what you already have. Is there music you can

hear, books you want to read, projects you want to complete, letters you would enjoy writing, friends you want to call? Do that today, instead of going out "in search of . . ."

3. Look around and consider how far you've come. Remember the days when you didn't know the Lord, when you were at ground zero. Think of how far he's brought you and rejoice in that.

The key to contentment is *to consider.* Consider who you are and be satisfied with that. Consider what you have and be satisfied with that. Consider what God's doing and be satisfied with that. You will be amazed at how much more comfortable you'll feel with yourself.

Finally, consider this: If contentment cannot be found within yourself, you'll never find it.

"Lord, make me content with who I am, what I have, and where I find myself. Because it is here, at this point, that you will meet me and, if necessary, change me. Amen."

A Castle in Italy

Marilyn Meberg

"If you, then, though you are evil,
know how to give good gifts to your
children, how much more will your
Father in heaven give good gifts
to those who ask him!"

MATTHEW 7:11

"You want to get married in Italy?! Good grief, Beth, why? No one could be there . . . what about your friends? Don't you want more people to be there cheering you on than just our small immediate family? Mercy . . . Italy!"

Slowly, very slowly, Beth began to sell me on the idea. Her logic turned out to be pretty convincing! Steve's parents were going to be in Udine, Italy, for six months. Steve and Beth reasoned that getting married during his parents' stay there would be perfect timing. After some investigation, I realized that flying there for a small wedding would probably be even less expensive than a full-blown wedding in

111

the States. I began to soften.

But the clincher came when Beth explained, "You know, Mom, I've never liked doing what everyone else does . . . it's boring. And you also know I've never wanted a traditional wedding. But more important, Mom, Dad isn't here to walk me down the aisle. Somehow being in an entirely different environment will make that reality less painful for me."

That did it . . . I was sold.

Beth and Steve were married in the "Castello Formentini" in Gorizia, Italy, on November 28, 1991. This fifteenth-century castle is utterly spectacular. Located on the border of what was once Yugoslavia, it has been renovated into a resort hotel complete with golf course. Interestingly enough, the renovations have not tampered in the slightest with its fifteenth-century charm.

After a sweetly Christ-centered service performed by the Soule's pastor from Udine, we retired to a stone-walled banquet room complete with gorgeous works of art and a crackling fire. We and the twenty other guests embarked upon a traditional Italian wedding feast that went on for five hours. All of this may sound a bit ostentatious, but if you can believe it, the dinner cost less than if we had had the American version of slightly stale wedding cake with chocolate mousse filling, preceded by cucumber and cream cheese canapés.

Watching Beth's radiant face in the midst of these magical festivities pleased me enormously. I thought how glad I was for her love of the different and unique and how grateful I was that God had so beautifully orchestrated this memorable event. After all, he too loves the different and unique, and he wants us to be true to our own peculiarities. God planted in Beth desires for her wedding ceremony that were uniquely her own, and I'm glad I honored them.

I am so grateful for God's provision not only for our basic needs but also for those that are occasionally far outside the norm. Sometimes I forget the sweet truth that God's Father-heart delights in giving good gifts to his children.

"Heavenly Father, thank you for those gifts you give us that are out of the ordinary and far beyond our expectations. There is no limit to your creativity, no limit to your generosity, and no limit to your pleasure in being our Father. Thank you that I am the daughter of the eternal King. Amen."

TWENTY-FIVE WAYS TO MAKE YOUR DAY

Barbara Johnson

"I have told you this so that
my joy may be in you and
that your joy may be complete."

JOHN 15:11

Give yourself a gift today: be present with yourself. God is. Enjoy your own personality. God does.

You are going to make it through whatever is on your plate. You are not only a survivor; you are a winner. Here are twenty-five fun, sometimes foolish, always productive ways to put a smile on your face. Make your day!

- Do the first drudgerous job on your list with a smile. Reward yourself by listening to a great piece of music.
- Prepare for surprises: life's most treas-

ured moments come unannounced.
- Clean and organize one drawer in your house.
- Write a note to someone you don't know well just to say, *"Hi, how are you?"*
- Start a journal if you don't already have one. Write down five things you are thankful for today.
- Believe you deserve to be happy. Say, "I open my arms wide to the very best God has for me today!"
- Find something to laugh about today. If all else fails, go get a joke book from the library, call the funniest person you know, or read this: What do you get when you cross an insomniac, an agnostic, and a dyslexic? Answer: A person who lies awake at night trying to decide if there really is a doG.
- Do something artsy. Dance to Mozart. Redecorate one wall. Paint a picture. Write a poem.
- Smile at yourself in the mirror. Wink back.
- Protect your enthusiasm from the negativity of others. Avoid toxic people today. If you run into one anyway, treat yourself to a double latte.
- Take a warm loaf of bread to an elderly person or shut-in.

- Take a power nap.
- Think about this: If you were going to die tomorrow and were allowed to make only one phone call, who would you call and what would you say? Now, make that call.
- Remember this: If you cheat on your diet you gain in the "end."
- Make eye contact with every person you meet and give a hug to at least half of them.
- Relish small pleasures.
- Hold all things loosely and mean it when you say, *"Whatever, Lord!"*
- Pray for somebody who has offended you.
- Don't allow a problem to be solved to become more important than a person to be loved.
- Take the word *struggle* out of your vocabulary and replace it with the word *adventure*.
- Take one step toward mending a broken relationship.
- Know this: The present is what slips by us while we're pondering the past and worrying about the future. Live in the now.
- Remember when you were five years old and just finding out how wonderful

you were? Write down the first memory that comes to mind.

- Ask yourself: What am I doing today that will bring me closer to where I want to be tomorrow?
- If you don't like your circumstances, find a new way to think about them.

"My Gracious Father, thank you that you give me a choice every moment about how I feel and respond to life. May I refuse to wait for someone else, but instead make my own day. Amen."

MAKE SOMETHING WITH YOUR HANDS

Luci Swindoll

Make it your ambition to lead a
quiet life, to mind your own business
and to work with your hands, just as we
told you, so that your daily life may win
the respect of outsiders and so that you
will not be dependent on anybody.

1 THESSALONIANS 4:11–12

I can't tell you how much I love that verse!
First of all, it actually says "mind your own
business." How many times have you wanted
to say that to someone but thought it might
be un-Christian, so you kept your mouth
shut . . . and here it is, *in print*. (I hasten to
add that it will be wiser if you let the other
person find that verse for herself rather than
suggesting she apply it in her life.)

Second, I appreciate any mandate that encourages me to work with my hands because

I heard that injunction so often as a child, from my mother. Bored with my little life, I would go to her in the desperation that only a ten-year-old can feel and beg her to tell me what to do. "Make something with your hands," she'd say, then suggest what that something might be. A greeting card. A painting. A mask. A little basket out of toothpicks or popsicle sticks. A schoolbook cover. She even suggested on one occasion that I help her make peanut brittle, which ended in utter disaster. I knew something was wrong when I attempted to lift the spoon out of the pot full of ingredients and everything came with it: peanuts, brittle, pot, and all. "Maybe we could call this modern art instead of candy?" I queried.

As I grew older, this love of handmade things grew with me. I could never get my fill of anything that permitted me to create or invent something from my own mind and hands and imagination. When I learned that Betsy, a friend from my early days at Mobil Oil, was extremely competent with knitting, I asked her to tell me what all she had made. She mesmerized me with stories of how she used to sit in dark movie houses, watching the film and following the plot, yet all the while knitting up a storm on some sweater or pair of socks she later sold to a little boutique in her hometown of Nashua, New Hampshire. I was amazed at the extent of her prowess.

"Do you think *I* could learn to knit?" I asked one day in complete candor. "Of course," she replied, "anybody can learn it. It's just the mastering of a skill. What would you like to make?" When I informed her I had always wanted a cashmere coat, she swallowed hard and suggested I might want to start with a pot holder. "Fine," I agreed, knowing full well I would get the hang of it in no time and by winter would indeed be wearing a coat of my own making.

Well, needless to say, knitting was a lot harder than I had imagined. Without my permission my hands clenched as I knitted and pearled away, and as the yarn tightened I ended up with an item that resembled a hockey puck instead of a pot holder. Betsy tried to encourage me and even offered to take over for me (which prompted my thoughts to go to the "mind your own business" part of the verse I referred to earlier).

Several months down the road, I finally admitted that proficiency in the skill of knitting was not to be. I kept that little hockey puck for years, however, as a reminder of the fun I had during those days of laughing and learning with Betsy. I may not have a cashmere coat, but I have lots of greeting cards, little paintings, masks, and handmade baskets. And I treasure them all.

God invites us to express our uniqueness and have fun by making things with our hands. These things don't have to be big or elaborate or even "correct," but making them should provide solace and personal fulfillment. Handmade things should reflect us: a fine meal, a garden patch, a beautiful quilt, a backdrop for a play, a piece of music, a poem, a letter. The idea is to keep our hands busy with meaningful activity so that we develop inside ourselves, depending upon the Lord and not on others for endorsement or approbation. May God help us to express and define ourselves in our one-of-a-kind way.

"Lord, remind me that I don't need the approval of someone else as long as you approve of me. May the way I live my life and the works of my hands reflect your glory and bring praise to you. Amen."

Write It Down

Luci Swindoll

"Remember that you were slaves
in Egypt and that the LORD your God
brought you out of there with a mighty
hand and an outstretched arm."

DEUTERONOMY 5:15

In the wee hours of my childhood mornings when I would come, sleepy-eyed, from my bedroom, there would be my mother, in prayer or Bible study. That picture of her sitting on her bed is impressed on my mind forever. In one hand she'd have her Bible and in the other, a notebook — or as she called it, "My Promise Book." Mother kept a record in that book of what God was teaching her, people she was praying for, issues she was concerned about, neighbors she wanted to see come to Christ. Every day she journaled her thoughts, feelings, God's promises to her, the words to hymns she found encouraging, poetry, and prayers. Mother's notebooks were a tremendous encouragement to her faith.

Now, many years later, they are an encouragement to me. After Mother's death, I kept her notebooks and, through the years, have referred to them on occasion. I cannot tell you how much they have taught me about her and about life. For example, I found written the fourth stanza of the hymn, "Oh Zion Haste":

Give of thy sons, to bear the message
   glorious;
Give of thy wealth to speed them on their
   way;
Pour out thy soul for them in prayer
   victorious;
And all thy spending Jesus will repay.

My mother wrote that, my mother prayed that, my mother did that. When I look at my brothers, both in lifetime Christian ministry, I realize my mother's impact on them (dare I say, on the world) is immeasurable. And to me, Mother modeled the importance of writing down my thoughts and concerns. I've journaled off and on my whole life, and for eleven years I have journaled *every day.*

My journals chronicle my joys and sorrows, progression and regression, trends, desires, regrets, and promises to myself (some kept, some broken). In various ones I have written prayers, songs, and poetry, and I've drawn pictures or used stickers on many of the pages. As I look back over them from time to time, I'm reminded that I was once "a slave in Egypt" and that God redeemed me and put a new song in my mouth and a spring in my step. He continually extends himself toward me, and I read of that over and over in those now yellowed pages.

There are many benefits to journaling, but for me one stands out above all the rest. I put a premium upon knowing one's self, and the blank pages of a journal give me a place to become better acquainted with me. I can explore my own feelings and questions, or come to grips with my own confusion or angst. I can cry as I write, or laugh. I can sort through my life's experiences and gain understanding about myself. I can privately wrestle with personal issues and conflicts.

None of this is an end in itself. Rather, it is my most effective tool for working through life's experiences and all the matters that concern me. Baring my soul in this manner takes me beyond a superficial, shallow existence or relationship with the Lord. I come to him with my eyes wide open and with understanding about myself. I am completely transparent with what I bring to him; consequently, it makes my relationship with him sweeter and far more intimate. In short, it helps me grow.

If you have never journaled, please don't let all this scare you. Don't be intimidated. Start where you are. Give it a try. Get a notebook. Take some time. See what happens. I think you'll surprise yourself with what comes out of your heart and mind. You don't have to be a "writer" — just let your thoughts, dreams, feelings, and prayers flow from you onto that page in your notebook. Nobody's going to see it but you. Be honest and real. And remember, you're not talking to yourself, but to the One who made you, loves you unconditionally, and receives you blameless.

"Lord, I praise you for the way you work in my life. Thank you for giving me the freedom to bare my soul to you anytime, in any way. I am awed by the fact that you want to commune with me, exactly as I am. Give me the courage to always be honest with you. Amen."

A Mirror Image

Marilyn Meberg

So God created man in his own image,
in the image of God he created him;
male and female he created them.

GENESIS 1:27

As an only child I never experienced the mirroring that often comes with having a sibling — you know, that catching a body gesture or tone of voice that wasn't mine but still looked or sounded a lot like mine. My childhood fantasy was to have an identical twin. In fact, I used to pretend I had a twin; in my imagination we talked alike, looked alike, and behaved alike.

I don't know the source of my desire for a twin other than the sense of isolation I occasionally felt as an only child in small rural communities. I wonder if in some way I thought an identical twin would validate my existence, assure me that "Yes, you are who you are and yes, you are there." (This sounds a bit neurotic, Marilyn . . .)

I thought I'd outgrown my "mirror-neurosis" until I met my Aunt Wilda for the first time about six years ago. She is my father's "baby sister." We don't look anything alike, but what startled me into a kind of primal recognition was her approach to life. As we were having dinner together in my home, Aunt Wilda, at my request, began to tell some of her early life experiences.

Her unbridled enthusiasm, zest for minor mischief as well as preference for the fast-paced life stirred in me a sense of having met my twin. What cinched that sense was her admission of her driving record. With twinkling Irish blue eyes she told me she was not proud of the fact that she continually got speeding tickets; but, she said, "Marilyn, how in the world do people manage to stay within the speed limit . . . it's simply too slow!" Responding with a hug of instant kinship, I began to share my own driving history and penchant for speeding.

Her response to my string of confessions was to pronounce, "There's no hope for you, Marilyn. Let me tell you why." She then told me how, shortly before Christmas one year, she had been pulled over by a policeman just outside her hometown of Toronto, Canada. He checked her license and insurance papers, then asked if she knew how fast she'd been going. Her response was, "Well, not as fast as I'd like . . . there are simply too many cars on the road!"

"Mrs. Johnson, I see by our computerized printout that you have quite a record of speeding tickets."

"Yes, I do, but that's not because I want them."

"What are the chances of your simply driving more slowly?"

"Probably not good."

"May I ask how old you are, Mrs. Johnson?"

"Eighty-two."

"I suppose it wouldn't do much good if I gave you a ticket then, would it?"

"I doubt it."

He patted her shoulder, told her to take care of herself, and said he hoped he would never have occasion to stop her again. She cheerfully replied, "I wouldn't mind that a bit. You are a lovely young man."

Concluding her story, she explained, "So you see, Marilyn, some things never change. You simply have 'speed genes'; you were probably born with them!"

I do not for one moment condone speeding and then excusing it by claiming, "I can't help it; it runs in the family." My point here is that there is sometimes an almost mysterious sense of the "ah-ha" when we meet people that seem to so perfectly mirror portions of ourselves. That experience provides a companionable feeling of oneness and kinship.

What is even more mysterious and provides an even greater sense of the "ah-ha" is the fact that we have been created in God's image. Jesus, who said "if you have seen me you have seen the Father," experienced every feeling, every nuance of emotion, every temptation on this earth that you and I do. If this truth is a reality to us, we can't help but be humbled by his graciousness in continually working to conform us to his image. What an awesome privilege that in our rebellious state he loves us and welcomes us always as part of the family — not because of what we do, but because of what he did on the cross.

When we look into the mirror, may we see more and more of him.

"Lord, what a mark of love and grace to be created in your image! And what grace you extend to us as you call us 'children of God.'

Enable us to talk like you, act like you, and even think like you as your Spirit refines us and molds us ever more into your image. Amen."

SPIRITUAL WHITE-OUT

Barbara Johnson

If we confess our sins, he is faithful
and just and will forgive us our sins
and purify us from all unrighteousness.

1 JOHN 1:9

Have you ever used that little bottle of stuff
called White-Out? It does a fantastic job of
erasing a mistake. With a dab of a brush, the
wrong letters you just typed disappear,
leaving a fresh white space for you to fill with
what is right.

Many years ago I had a job scheduling
doctor's appointments. When someone
would cancel or reschedule, the marks
would make the book look messy. That
bothered me. I'd have to write over or under
the name to be replaced, or sometimes in
the margins or in big letters right over the
scratched-out scribble.

Then one day I discovered that White-
Out was the miracle I'd been looking for to

131

keep the doctor's books orderly and professional looking. I'd paint a nice clean space where the client's name had been. At the end of the day, every page was neat and clean. Instead of messy columns there'd be straight and easy-to-read names for the receptionist in the office.

I used to call White-Out my 1 John 1:9 stuff because it would blot out the mess and leave a clean place — just like God does with our sins. We all need that spiritual White-Out to make us white as snow (Isaiah 1:18). It reminds us we can all have a clean fresh start every day. Every dawn is a new beginning from the very first rays of sunshine or light in the sky. No, we can't go back and change the past, but God can make each space in our lives new. One thing God cannot see is our sin because it is covered by his special White-Out: the blood of Jesus.

Sometimes we want to escape the space we're in — the circumstances of our lives. We'd like to live on the coast if we live in the Midwest, or in the mountains if we live in a city. We think if we did, our lives wouldn't be such a mess. Maybe we'd like to be in a different family, married to a different spouse, working at a different job, or dealing with a different problem — anything but the one we have.

Sometimes we'd like to cancel God's appointments for us: Why must we go through *this* particular trial? Look *this* particular way? Be saddled with *this* particular thorn in the flesh? We'd like to reschedule some of our afflictions for another day, put off our troubles until a more convenient time. Often we try, but usually we find ourselves in a bigger mess than ever.

Our life appointment book is best presided over by the Great Physician and his miraculous White-Out. Each of our lives is an unfolding drama. Moment by moment and day by day, he enters the details of our lives in his book. There are times when he captures each tear in his medicine bottle like it says in Psalm 56:8 (LB). I believe he pours them back on our lives as laughter another day.

Always, when things go wrong because we struggle against the way things are, God comes along to White-Out our sin of rebellion. Our lack of faith. Unforgiveness. Complacency. That one little bottle does it all.

So, settle into the grace of his presence right now. He knows your name. It is written in his book. He knows all the days appointed for you. And you can bet on it: when he needs to, he knows how to use the White-Out for his glory and your great good. Then he writes in the clean space the name of the one through whom you have been made righteous: Jesus Christ.

"*Dear Heavenly Father, our Great Physician and our Savior, thank you for the blood of Jesus that cleanses us from all our sin. Thank you for the Holy Spirit who fills us with your peace so we can rest in our circumstances. Thank you for the promises of forgiveness and righteousness in your Son's name. Amen.*"

Heavenbound

Patsy Clairmont

Now we know that if the
earthly tent we live in is destroyed,
we have a building from God,
an eternal house in heaven,
not built by human hands.

2 Corinthians 5:1

I'm enthralled with books that have great opening lines. Oh, sure, the rest of the book must strike a flame, but a sizzling opener sparks my interest. One of my all-time favorites is a book extract from 1909 by Mark Twain entitled "Captain Stormfield's Visit to Heaven." The opening line reads, "Well, when I had been dead about thirty years, I began to get a little anxious."

When I read that line, I was hooked. I laughed aloud and then wanted to know what was going on in this story. It seems Captain Stormfield had died and was hurled immediately outside of earth's orbit, spinning through space headed for heaven. The journey was taking a smidgen longer (thirty years) than he had anticipated. I actually became lost in my attempts to stay with the Captain's journey, but I never forgot that zinger of an opening line.

Imagine being outside of our earthly orbit free-floating toward the celestial shore. Whee! It sounds delicious. Sort of how I felt as a little girl when I would swing a little too high and my tummy would be tickled by a swarm of fluttering butterflies. Very exciting, plus some. To be Jesus-bound will be heavenly, but for now we remain on terra firma. This means that learning to stay in our own orbit is essential.

Hurling through space is one thing; hurling through life could be catastrophic. Hurling suggests we thrust ourselves forward regardless of anything or anyone in our path.

Consider the disciple, orbital Peter, a fellow who had trouble keeping his feet on solid ground. He was always flinging himself into thin air. Remember when Jesus was arrested and Peter hurled himself toward the guard, rearranging the guard's anatomy with his sword? Jesus, knowing Peter was outside of his orbit, stepped in and healed the astonished guard. Peter, despite his good intentions, wasn't helping the situation or Jesus.

When we step out of our orbit into someone else's, we don't help either. Knowing when to stay back and when to step forward can be a hard call if we don't have well-defined boundaries. I'm sure Peter thought he was doing the right — even the valiant — thing. But he wasn't.

I'm a Peter. At least in the sense that I've stepped, sometimes rushed, and yes, even hurled myself into others' orbits. Even lopped off a few ears (at least it probably felt like it to those involved). In fact, I remember far too clearly a situation some years ago where I felt led (ugh) to inform (even though she had not asked) a dear woman of some of her character flaws. She was gracious even though I had hurled myself into her orbit uninvited. This event still brings me pain as I recall it. I have prayed that Jesus intervene on her behalf and heal that unnecessary wound I inflicted.

I know the Lord has forgiven me, but I don't want him to release me from the regret I feel. It serves as a sort of orbital monitoring device keeping me in my designated space. For I have found there is plenty for me to do in my own solar system without attempting adjustments in someone else's.

Do you remember the television show from the 1970s called *Lost in Space*? On board the spaceship was a shallow, self-consumed professor whom everyone in the TV audience loved to hate. He exemplified all of our worst traits, always causing a stir and blundering his way through everyone else's orbits.

We, too, become offensive when we lack wisdom, sensitivity, and good judgment toward those around us. We need to respect others' space and clean up our own orbit. Then, one day, one glorious day, in the twinkling of an eye, we will be out of here — not lost in space, but headed through space toward Home!

"Thank you, Lord, that we are glory bound. Hallelujah!"

A Place for You

Luci Swindoll

"In my Father's house are
many rooms; if it were not so,
I would have told you. I am going
there to prepare a place for you."

JOHN 14:2

What a promise! Jesus is preparing *a place for me*. My own room. This is really important to me, and here's why: *I have to have a place.*

In my adult life I have moved about ten different times, and in every case I notice a pattern. The first thing I do, long before I unpack everything, is prepare a place for myself. It goes like this: I move the most comfortable chair over to one corner and put a table beside that chair with a radio, lamp, the book I'm reading, and a bouquet of flowers. I hang a painting on the wall behind the chair, enclose it with either a screen or stack of boxes, toss a throw rug on the floor, and count it my haven. There may be chaos in every other corner of the house but not in this one. I have a place to go to escape. Blessed retreat.

When I travel I also notice a pattern. It goes like this: I check into a room, and even if I'm going to be there only one night, I unpack my entire suitcase and put my stuff in the drawers and on the bathroom counter. I put away the luggage and place the little treasures I brought from home strategically around the room: my Bible, my journal, my music, my tiny little leather-bound world atlas . . . all stuff I might need. In short, I prepare a place for me.

When I board an airplane I again notice a pattern. It goes like this: The minute the *Fasten Seat Belt* sign goes off I open my carry-on bag and take out my stuff. I surround myself with my books, a newspaper, a magazine, a postcard I want to write, and I prepare a little place for me for the duration of the trip. I all but hang a little cross-stitched "Home Sweet Home" sign on the food tray.

Call me eccentric (and many do) but it is my way, and I'm glad to know it's God's way, too. *He* is preparing a place for me.

Our "place" provides so much . . . not only shelter but also a setting to be alone or together with those we love. Our place is an expression of who we are. It reflects our inner person.

Inevitably, when the four of us on the Joyful Journey team arrive in a city, it's only a matter of time until we all congregate in one of our rooms. This is never planned beforehand, nor orchestrated by anyone, but it always happens. We gravitate to a quiet place to fellowship with one another. You probably do the same thing with your friends. You use your "place" to be with others.

But let me ask you this: have you discovered the value of being alone in your own place? The author Leo Buscaglia writes, "We all need our separate worlds, apart from others, where we can quietly retire for regrouping, for getting back in touch with ourselves. We need this personal solitary place as a pleasant alternative to our more public lives. We must treasure this part of our existence as much as we do the more social part. Then, when loneliness comes, we will have that special place to fall back upon."[*]

Oh, how true! Jesus himself sets the example. Consider John 6:15, where it says

[*]Leo Buscaglia, *Bus Nine to Paradise* (New York: William Morrow and Co., 1986), 142.

"Jesus . . . withdrew again to a mountain by himself." In the Old Testament we are instructed by the Lord to "come away, my lover"(Song of Songs 8:14).

Your idea of creating a place to be with yourself may not be the same as mine, and that's fine. But I can promise you that until you learn that solitude is your friend and not your enemy, until you are comfortable "staying in your own orbit," you will have little to give anyone else. Buscaglia says every individual has the "sacred responsibility of becoming a complete person." When that happens, having a place all our own will have its greatest value. In it we can celebrate our uniqueness and rejoice with our Savior.

"Jesus, just as you are ultimately preparing a room for me for all eternity, help me to have the wisdom to create a special spot to be with you . . . to be alone . . . to engage in meaningful communion with others. Amen."

My Heart Is Wallpapered to God's

Barbara Johnson

"Though he slay me,
yet will I hope in him."

Job 13:15

Snug. Secure. Attached. Connected. Immovable. Bonded. Superglued.

These words describe the way sticky stuff magically takes two separate objects and makes them one. I like these words. They describe my relationship to God as I've gone through some very tough times.

You know those little spongy tape strips you can buy to attach stuff? I bought some to stick plastic pegs to the inside of a cupboard door so I could hang up washcloths. Once I got them on I changed my mind and decided to hang the washcloths somewhere else. I pulled and pried at the pegs, but could not get them loose. Bill tried, too, but he didn't succeed either. Finally one day when my son was visiting I asked him to help me. He managed to get the pegs off, but those sticky spongy pieces of tape are still adhered to the inside of the door!

The sticky stuff looks tacky, but I decided to let it remind me of how God never gives up on us no matter how hard we try to get ourselves loose. God does not let go. That doesn't mean he controls everything we do. It doesn't mean he puts a bridle on us and leads us by the nose. He gives each one of us free will and common sense and a spirit that can communicate with his. When we go through afflictions, he allows us to choose our response. But no matter what our response may be, he sticks around to the bitter end.

Sometimes I think God is smiling while I rant and rave and pound on the floor objecting to the unfairness of life. It's like God is saying, "Come on, Barbara, is that the best you can do? I can take more than that."

God has a better sense of humor than any of us. He may laugh at our tantrums — in a good-natured way. Other times I think he just ignores them because while we're begging him to change things he sees the bigger picture.

Once I watched a little boy playing on a huge weathered tree adrift at the lakeshore. The boy thought the waves on the lake were pulling the tree away from shore. He kept crying, "Daddy, Daddy, help, it's moving." I felt kind of sorry for the little guy because the rocking of the waves must have felt powerful to him. But his dad, who was reading the Sunday paper in the sun a few feet away on the beach, knew that huge tree wasn't going anywhere. He let his son whine, not out of indifference, but just because he saw the bigger picture. He was nearby. He expected his boy to take solace in that security. He could be there in a heartbeat if needed.

I thought, *How much like me and my heavenly Father.* God gives me credit for being able to take more than I think I can take. He wants me to take comfort in the fact that he is close. He isn't going anywhere, and no matter how scary things get, he won't come unglued.

I guess that's what Job was feeling when he spoke about trusting God when the worst Job thought could happen did happen. I guess that's what Abraham was feeling when he took his son up on the mountain to make the ultimate sacrifice to the Lord. What emotional battles these men must have fought! Their words of faith did not come easily. They were wrested from the raw material of pain and loss.

Our afflictions are designed not to break us but to bend us toward the eternal and the holy. God sticks with us through it all. One lady who wrote to me summed it up this way: "My heart is wallpapered to God's heart."

The apostle Paul said nothing can separate us from God's love, no matter how we might try to pry ourselves loose. "Who shall separate us from the love of Christ?" Paul asks. "Shall trouble or hardship or persecution or famine or nakedness or danger or sword?" No, he assures us, "Neither death nor life, neither angels nor demons, neither the present nor the future, nor any powers, neither height nor depth, nor anything else in all creation, will be able to separate us from the love of God that is in Christ Jesus our Lord" (Romans 8:35, 38–39).

There you go.

"Dear God, thanks for sticking with me like glue. I'm so glad you have wallpapered my heart to yours. Amen."

"WHATEVER, LORD"

Relinquishing Your Agendas

"However, Lord"

Patsy Clairmont

"Be it done to me
according to your word."

LUKE 1:38 (nasb)

When Les asks me where I want to eat, I often will say, "I don't care, wherever." Then he will say, "What about the Inn?"

My immediate reply is, "No, I don't want to go there. Anywhere but there."

"Okay," he will respond, "then how about the Fiesta?"

"No, not the Inn or the Fiesta, but anywhere else."

By now we both know I didn't really mean "wherever," and it will shorten the process if I just tell him where I'm willing to go.

I have had this same conversation with the Lord. I tell him in prayer I will do whatever he asks of me. Then he sends some rascals into my life, and I'm irritated. When I said "whatever," I guess I meant as long as it's not too inconvenient, not too disruptive to my schedule, and not too long-term costly. The truth is, my "Whatever, Lord" is really more a "However, Lord." "I'll do it, Lord; however, could you make it another time, a little easier, a more agreeable person, and to my liking?" I think the true "Whatever, Lord" usually comes after we have exhausted all our bright ideas, we are spent, and we have finally moved to a point of relinquishment.

Scripture gives us some beautiful examples of "Whatever, Lord" people who didn't add howevers and didn't have to come to their wit's end to trust him explicitly.

Consider the Virgin Mary's response to the angel's visitation. A maiden with her whole life before her is asked to risk scandal, misunderstanding, lunacy charges, and possibly stoning. Mary, however, doesn't see it as a risk but as an honor to be chosen (even if it included scandal, misunderstanding, and so forth). We read her powerful "Whatever, Lord" in the gospel of Luke: "Behold, the bondslave of the Lord; be it done to me according to your word" (1:38 NASB).

Now that's trust. How impressive that such a young woman would respond immediately to a request never before made of anyone. It wasn't as if others had ever been in this situation and Mary could use their experience to guide her. When the angel Gabriel extended God's incredible invitation, Mary was flying solo with no previous experience. She also was so-low in her response, for Scripture tells us her heart was humble.

Mary's reply surfaces another insight about a "Whatever, Lord" person: that individual has humility. Relinquishment (when I give up on me and give in to him) and humility (lowliness of mind) are rare attributes. It almost sounds as if these two qualities depend on each other, doesn't it? Like you can't have one without the other? But wait, there's more . . .

Remember Abigail? She was the wife of Nabal, a hard-hearted man who had no respect for authority. Nabal's arrogance and his unwillingness to extend gratitude to others placed Abigail, her family, and their workers' lives in jeopardy. David and his men had protected Nabal's shepherds and sheep from vandals. But when David asked if he and his men could share in the festivities of a feast day with Nabal, he rebuffed David. Abigail rushed to meet David, who had sharpened his sword in preparation to repay Nabal for his unneighborly attitude, and in an act of relinquishment and humility she presented her case. David was moved by this woman's passion to right wrongs and to protect him from making a foolish mistake. He not only honored her request to spare her household, but also, after the (natural) death of her husband, David made Abigail his wife. Her zealous entreaty, laced with humility and relinquishment, is found in 1 Samuel 25 and worth feasting your eyes on.

So we add passion to our "Whatever, Lord" list — passion to do what is honorable and therefore right in God's eyes. We "see" and hear Abigail's passion when she dismounts her donkey in David's presence, falls on her face before him, and says, "My lord, let the blame be on me alone" (1 Samuel 25:24).

Abigail's salutation disarmed David. I'm sure he anticipated a defensive attitude — one full of excuses from a scoundrel whom he did not plan to listen to. Instead, David comes upon a "Whatever, Lord" woman, an honorable woman with an impassioned plea. Rather than a whiny, self-centered request, Abigail demonstrates, by laying her life on the line, a warm concern for the welfare of all.

Relinquishment, humility, and passion: "A cord of three strands is not quickly broken" (Ecclesiastes 4:12).

Are you a "whatever" woman or a "however" woman?

How do you exhibit godly passion?

Who presents a picture of humility you can emulate?

What does the Lord want you to relinquish to him?

"Jesus, 'Whatever, Lord' is a scary prayer; yet we want to trust you, and so we risk . . . Whatever, Lord. Amen."

THIS IS NOT WHAT I HAD IN MIND

Luci Swindoll

In his heart a man plans his course
but the LORD determines his steps.

PROVERBS 16:9

One of the most delightful weekends I had spent since moving to California six months before was nearing an end as two teenage girls approached me while I was counting out my vitamins. "What are all those pills for?" one of them asked. "Well," I explained, "these two are for beautiful eyes, this one is for long willowy legs, that little one is for pearly, white teeth . . ." and as I was waxing on, the other girl interrupted me with, "Haven't been taking them long, have you?"

What a comeback! This girl was one sharp cookie. In fact, all twelve of them were.

The Pioneer Girl retreat had been filled

with laughter and hilarity, as well as sweet communion and meaningful interaction. And, to think . . . I almost missed it.

You see, Marilyn had signed me up to join her in teaching a class of Pioneer Girls on Wednesday nights at our church in Fullerton, California. I was not thrilled. I had done this to people but had never had it done to me. I remember signing up a fellow employee at Mobil Oil to play on the baseball team. I even volunteered her to be captain of the team, just to hear her try to worm out of it when the team captain phoned her. But somehow I had escaped this type of unsolicited commitment from my friends — until Marilyn came along.

Now, here I was, a teacher to these young teenage girls, who would look to me for spiritual and emotional guidance on Wednesday evenings. This was the *last* thing in life I wanted to do. I resisted mightily:

1. I'm not qualified . . . I've never taught this kind of class before.
2. I've got better things to do with my time, like watch the Wednesday night TV lineup.
3. I'm too tired after working all day.
4. The pay's too low (after all, I was volunteering).

I could come up with at least ninety-eight reasons why I didn't want to do this. But Marilyn had put my name on the dotted line to teach for a year, no less! I could have died, right after killing her.

But, as is always the case, God knew what I could not have known: that I *needed* this experience. I needed the opportunity to prepare for the Bible studies I would teach those young girls. I found that what I was teaching them was rubbing off on me. I got to know them, their parents, and their siblings. Before I knew it I was investing in their futures as they talked about their schoolwork, their boyfriends, their problems, their fears . . . on and on and on. As long as I would listen, they would talk. About everything. And, as I spent those hours with Marilyn (fairly early in our own relationship), I came to see what a fun, joyful, dear friend she was going to be.

God did several meaningful things in my life during that year, and I'm so glad I taught that class in spite of my initial resistance.

What are you resisting? Has God been nudging you into action and you've either said "no" repeatedly, or "well, maybe" so weakly that no one can hear it? I can tell you from my own experience, the very thing we say "no" to just might be God's blessing in disguise. He wants to bless us; he wants to mature us; he wants to get us out of our comfort zone.

The *last* thing you want to do just might be the best thing that ever happened to you. It might even be fun.

"How often I resist your bidding, Lord, and miss opportunities to enjoy your gifts. Because of my fear and insecurity, I hesitate; I look within instead of looking to you. Show me your agenda for today, God, and give me the grace and boldness to follow it. Surprise me with your wisdom and delights. Amen."

"THE PLAN"

Marilyn Meberg

In him we were also chosen,
having been predestined according
to the plan of him who works out
everything in conformity with
the purpose of his will.

EPHESIANS 1:11

During my last visit to Beth and Steve's house in Carmel, little Ian, Beth, and I drove to the neighboring town of Monterey so Beth could see Dr. Walker, her ob-gyn. Why? Because she's pregnant!

Am I excited? Does the sun shine daily in Palm Desert? I'm thrilled to death!

This is cutting it a bit close in some ways, though, because Ian will only be twenty-three months old when "she" arrives. I'm sure Ian's initial response will be to pack his little suitcase in disgust and move to Grandma's.

As they have talked over the unexpected

timing of her pregnancy, Beth and Steve have both had to walk through a few steps before relinquishing their agendas. Both feel Ian is a bit too young to have to relinquish his position as King Baby. The timing is not great for them financially; both had hoped to get a bit ahead or, more realistically, just catch up before another baby hit the scene. And Beth wanted one more year to see that Ian is as grounded as possible in this world of good times and bad before facing the inevitable sibling rivalry that comes when new kids arrive on board.

I don't think there's a human being schlepping through life that does not have a "plan" for how things will be. "We'll have two babies, a boy and a girl, who will be three years apart, and then after that . . ." There also is not a human being alive who has not experienced unexpected interruptions or unwanted alterations to "the plan." The one constant in life is change. Nothing stays the same, and the same is usually changed to something we don't recognize. We are in a continual cycle of beginnings, middles, and endings, and not always in that order. If we habitually resist that reality, we'll generally be distressed with life.

When I finally internalized the plan-shattering reality that Ken had cancer and that cancer was going to kill him, my mind reeled with a million arguments. "Now wait a minute . . . we were supposed to retire in ten years and take trips . . . I was going to surprise him with a golf cart on our thirtieth wedding anniversary . . . we're supposed to indulge and spoil grandchildren together . . . Ken was supposed to make gourmet dinners every Saturday night for the rest of our lives . . . Ken was supposed to always do the income taxes so I wouldn't ever even have to look at the forms . . . we were supposed to hold each other when we were cold, lonely, or simply loving. What about all that stuff, God?"

I have every invitation from the Father to fuss and complain about "the plan." However, if I stay in the fuss-complain mode and refuse to relinquish my agenda, I'll never have peace.

How do we truly give up our agendas? How do we genuinely say, "Not my will but yours, Lord"? For me, the answer to that question is found in my understanding of and acceptance of God's sovereignty. God "works out everything in conformity with the purpose of his will." All happenings on this earth and in my life are worked out in conformity with his purpose — not mine, but his. God's sovereignty is not an attribute of God but a prerogative of God. He does what he does.

What softens my response to what in my human understanding could seem autocratic of God is to remember the nature of God. The nature of God is love. For a rich reminder of this attribute of his, just look up all the verses on his love for you in a Bible concordance. It will soften your resistance and inspire a reciprocal love for him. His love is simply too great and too all-encompassing to step around.

Based on that love platform is the realization that I am not incidental in the grand scheme of things. In Ephesians 1:4–5, the apostle Paul tells us, "For he chose us in him before the creation of the world to be holy and blameless in his sight. In love he predestined us to be adopted as his sons through Jesus Christ, in accordance with his pleasure and will."

I am not an afterthought. All God's love-inspired preplanning for each of us is not haphazard or impersonal. His timing may throw me or his sovereign plan may grieve me, but I am always sheltered in his sovereign hand. Can I rest in that . . . can I quit resisting that? Not always, but that's my humanness interfering with my acceptance of his divineness.

Are Beth and Steve having an ill-timed baby? Not according to Ephesians 1:11. Did Ken die prematurely? Not according to Ephesians 1:11. Perhaps the more appropriate question is, "Will I accept his sovereign will in my life?" If I do, or when I do, I will have experienced his sovereign plan for my life.

"Lord, how frequently and mindlessly we kick against the very constraints you put in place for our growth and refinement. Remind those of us who get so caught up with the earthly that to do so is to miss the heavenly. Your plan for each of us is not one of earthly ease but of heavenly peace. Amen."

THE BIG LITTLE WORD: LET!

Luci Swindoll

He who has an ear, let him hear.

REVELATION 13:9

Last week I was in the grocery store and there was a mother and her little son in front of me, pushing their cart along. This kid was driving me crazy with his constant demands: "Let me hold that. Let me push the cart. Let me ride up there. Let me have the cookies. Let me see that box. Let me buy that candy. Let me pay the money." I'm telling you, I was standing there thinking, *Let me at that kid!* I wanted to say to that mother, "Why did you ever teach your son the word *let?* Didn't you know it would come to this? Don't you know what that word means?"

Let! That's one of the most powerful words in the English language. It says, "Allow me . . . permit me." It urges con-

163

sent. As I drove home from the store, I kept thinking about that word, and I realized it is used repeatedly in the Bible. In fact, when I got home, I looked up the number of times it could be found. Would you believe over nine hundred? I took time to check out some of the references and found that the "let verses" cover practically every mandate in the Christian life. Just listen to a few:

1 John 4:7	Let us love one another.
Hebrews 12:2	Let us fix our eyes on Jesus.
Colossians 4:6	Let your conversation be always full of grace.
Psalm 5:11	Let all who take refuge in you be glad.
Psalm 95:2	Let us come before him with thanksgiving.
Psalm 99:1	Let the nations tremble . . . let the earth shake.
Psalm 119:27	Let me understand the teaching of your precepts.
Proverbs 1:5	Let the wise listen and add to their learning.
Proverbs 3:3	Let love and faithfulness never leave you.
Romans 14:13	Let us stop passing judgment on one another.

| Galatians 6:9 | Let us not become weary in doing good. |
| Colossians 3:15 | Let the peace of Christ rule in your hearts. |

Here are only twelve references, and remember: there are over nine hundred! Choose any one of those and give it your consideration; you could be thinking about it for hours. Let (there's that word again!) me challenge you to do a personal Bible study on this simple, wonderful, powerful word. Look it up in your concordance, write down a reference, look up the verse, meditate on it, and ask God to make it real in your life.

I did that with Galatians 5:25 which says, "Let us keep in step with the Spirit." What does this mean to me today? To keep in step means to allow the Holy Spirit to guide my life. That requires from me a response that says, "Lord, I will go where *you* want me to go, I will do what *you* want me to do, I will be what *you* want me to be, because I trust *you* to keep me in step with you." This puts the responsibility in its proper place: on the shoulders of the Holy Spirit and not on mine. He does the guiding, I do the letting.

I wish I could see that little kid now. I think I would listen to him differently. Instead of seeing him as a nuisance, I might see him as a good reminder of what God wants to say to me: "Luci, *let me . . .*"

Next time you're in the grocery store and would like to throttle some demanding child, let him or her instead serve to remind you that God wants to get your attention. He wants to say to you, *"Let . . ."*

"Heavenly Father, give me an ear that can hear you in the simplest ways. As I go about my duties today, help me hear your voice in that of another's so I will let go of my will and direct my attention to yours. Let your light shine upon my path so each step I take will be guided by you. Amen."

FORGIVENESS MEANS GET OVER IT

Barbara Johnson

Be kind and compassionate to
one another, forgiving each other,
just as in Christ God forgave you.

EPHESIANS 4:32

When my third son, Larry, admitted he was a homosexual, I nearly lost my mind. My grief over Larry's behavior was very different from my grief over the deaths of my two older sons, one killed in Vietnam and the other hit by a drunk driver five years later. My grief over Larry was a deep crushing feeling in my chest, a kind of brokenness from which I thought I would never recover. As I've recounted in my book *Stick a Geranium in Your Hat and Be Happy!*, years accumulated under my sorrow, and with those years, I learned to be healthy even in my pain.

When Larry finally did recommit his life

to the Lord, we did a radio interview together for "Focus on the Family" with Dr. James Dobson. On that program, Larry said: "If we as Christians can purpose in our hearts to be kind and loving in all that we do and put away a condemning spirit, and learn the fear of the Lord, then surely the light of Christ will be able to shine in our disbelieving world, and restoration and revival will take root in the lives we touch on a daily basis."

Since that day, these words have been printed on Christmas cards and in church bulletins and shared by audio tape around the world. But before Larry could speak those words, I had to live them out for myself.

There is no way to silence the grief of having to mourn a loved one who has not died. Rage and confusion accompanied the broken-hearted pangs I suffered. I endured the long periods of Larry's absence and rebellion by remembering the good things.

Once when Larry was ten, he was assigned a solo in our church Christmas program. All week at home he'd practice by singing: "While shepherds washed their socks by night all seated on the ground, the angel of the Lord came down and said, 'Will you wash mine?' and said, 'Will you wash mine?' " I told him I'd give him five dollars to sing it like that in the program. (Of course, I was teasing.) He said, *never*. On the night of the program, however, Larry got up and sang it just like he'd practiced, reaping the audience's laughter and applause.

These kinds of memories kept me alive. But guilt had turned me into a recluse. My pain turned to depression. But just as my rope was fraying, I decided to let go of it altogether. I grew so tired of giving Larry to God and taking him back again that I decided to nail my son to the cross. In my imagination I took out a hammer and did just that. I told God, "If Larry never comes home and I never see him again — whatever, Lord!" This is the prayer of relinquishment.

That is when forgiveness took root in my heart. Forgiveness is powerful — not only the ability to forgive, but the ability to be forgiven. I did see Larry again. I asked him to forgive me for the times I hadn't shown understanding or love.

I've seen teenagers wearing T-shirts that say, "Get Over It!" I think Christians should take the lead when it comes to getting over offenses and moving on. Oh, I know, sometimes this is a huge, overwhelming task. But even in long-term grief there is a way to bring closure and to rise above the rage, the guilt, the pain. In Christ this is possible.

Perhaps if the *Guinness Book of World Records* had a section about the world's greatest forgivers, we might see the name of one shining Christian after another. I wonder if Barbara Johnson's name might make it down at the bottom of the list? Would your name be there?

Challenge yourself to stretch further than you thought you ever could! Take the first step in the long direction of forgiving those who have offended you, hurt you, maimed you for life.

"Get over it"? Perhaps Christians should have thought of this first. Well, maybe they did!

"Dear Lord Jesus, we commit ourselves and our loved ones into your hands. We want to be good forgivers — expert forgivers like you are. What we cannot manage to forgive this moment, help us to move toward one degree at a time. Amen."

GOD'S PLUMP, JUICY RAISINS

Barbara Johnson

Blessed are those whose
strength is in you, who have
set their hearts on pilgrimage.
As they pass through the
Valley of Baca, they make it
a place of springs; the autumn
rains also cover it with pools.

PSALM 84:5–6

Recently I spoke at the Raisin Festival in Dinuba, California, the Raisin Capital of the World. I learned a lot about raisins there and watched how they turn grapes into raisins that are juicy and sweet.

These raisin professionals use a unique process unlike anything I'd imagined. First, they take only the best California grapes. Then they give them the "spa treatment": the grapes are bathed in hot water followed by twenty-four hours of controlled dehydration in warm air. Finally, the raisins are cooled and gently washed again in warm water before being bundled in convenient packages. The process entails great care heating the initial hot-water bath, gradually cooling the water, then heating it again to insure plump, moist raisins. Other packers, they told us, dry the grapes in the sun, with questionable results.

I'm like a grape. When I'm left in the sun to dry, I lose my resilience, too. I end up washed-out with questionable nourishing qualities. Let's face it: We all get parched in the deserts of life. We need springs and pools to refresh us, to make us plump with faith and moist with good deeds.

Someone once said, "Christians are like tea. Their strength comes out in hot water." I say, "Christians are like grapes, too. In hot water, we get sweeter and juicier and prove that we can endure the process of life."

I don't know about you, but I sure don't want to end up an old pious prune. Nor do I want to end up like one of those hard little crusty raisins I sometimes find at the bottom of a box. I'll gladly take the hot water God puts me in because I know *he knows* I need it. Sometimes a good soaking brings out stuff I didn't know I had in me, like courage, dignity, compassion.

As for the controlled dehydration, I figure that's pretty much like God's love and patience. Twenty-four hours a day he's there, backing me up, guiding me forward, ready to speak, ready to listen. Never giving me more than I can bear. Always giving me just enough to make me sweeter than I was the day before.

Like the raisin producers, God knows we need cooling, too. Sometimes he cools our heels. There are times when love walks out the door and he doesn't stop it from going. Maybe a friend moves out of town and he lets her leave. A job ends. A child rebels. The pages of the Bible stare at us blankly. He lets our passions cool off — even the spiritual ones. Even the seemingly good ones, the ones we thought were from him and would last forever. Only he knows why. But he's perfecting his raisins.

Just in time, he heats up the process again. Someone touches us with an encouraging word of kindness. A stranger gives us a warm smile. We share sympathetic warm tears or hear echoes of warm-hearted laughter when we least expect it. Maybe someone makes us chuckle in spite of ourselves or even at ourselves. God doesn't leave us cold, isolated, abandoned. He doesn't let us cool one minute too long.

I don't know about you, but I intend to cooperate with God in his work as Master Raisin Maker. I've tasted of the Lord's fruit, and it is good. Sweeter than honey. Ready to serve. And that's what I intend to do: serve him and others. I'm raisin' my prayers and praise to his beautiful will.

"Dear Lord, there is none like you. No one can compete with your love and care in preparing your children to nourish the languishing world. Here I am, Lord: pick me! Choose me to be one of your sweet, plump, juicy ones. I'll gladly serve you. Amen."

WHERE ARE YOU?

Patsy Clairmont

Jesus Christ is the same
yesterday and today and forever.

HEBREWS 13:8

A woman recently wrote to me asking, "How does one find God?" Hmm. Great question, isn't it? God is sort of like the wind in that we see evidence of his presence; yet he isn't easily grasped. We can't touch him, yet we can feel his presence as surely as our own. We don't hear an audible voice, yet at times he speaks as definitely and clearly as anyone we've heard.

I see God's fingerprints in his handiwork: a sunrise, a shooting star, a lilac bush, and a newborn's smile. I observe a measure of his strength in a hurricane, an earthquake, a thunderbolt. I see his creativity in a kangaroo, the Grand Canyon, and a blue-eyed, red-headed baby. I detect his humor in a porpoise, a cactus, and a two-year-old's

175

twinkling eyes. I am aware of his mysteriousness when I consider the Trinity, the solar system, and his desire to be in communion with us. "What is man that you are mindful of him?" (Psalm 8:4).

But how do we find God? Sometimes we search him out, and sometimes he "finds" us. Every time we think of God it is because he first had us on his mind. The Lord is always the initiator. He has been from the beginning (Genesis 1:1), and he will be to the end (Revelation 1:7). So know that once you have invited him to enter your life, you are on his mind and he is in your heart.

The Lord settled into our hearts is another mystery. How could we, with our tiny hearts — not to mention our itsy-bitsy brains — house him who is without beginning or end (Revelation 1:8)? We could not — aside from his miraculous power and his desire to inhabit us.

I have learned that sometimes we will be aware of his closeness and sometimes we won't. At times we experience the sweetness of God's nearness and at other times the frightening loneliness of his distance. The Lord hasn't changed locations, but we might have become caught up in our own agendas and forgotten his presence and availability. Other times the Lord will be silently still (scary) for holy purposes (awesome) we don't understand (frustrating), yet . . . (hallelujah).

How does one find God? Perhaps we need to rest from our pursuit of the Almighty and allow him to reveal himself to us. This is not to say we should stop any honorable efforts to find him such as in church, Bible study, or fellowship. On the contrary, these endeavors shore us up while we wait. But in the midst of our journey, we need to allow him to lead us even to lonely terrain. Surprisingly, our loneliness can cause us to pursue the Lord even more.

How does one find God? He is in our prayers guiding our words, he is in our songs as we worship him, and he is filling our mouths when we comfort a friend or speak wisdom to someone who needs hope. Sometimes we can search so hard for the miraculous we miss the obvious reality of his ever-present nearness. Count your blessings. He is in them, too.

We can't command the Lord into our awareness. He is King; we are his beloved subjects. When our hearts are tenderly responsive ("Whatever, Lord") and it suits his greater plan, then the Lord will lift the thin veil that separates us. And we will be stunned to realize that he has been closer than our own breath all along.

By the way, it has been my experience that I keep refinding him, which has helped to define me. You, too, may lose track of your faith. Remember, it is never too late to step back on the path.

"Lord, who fills the universe and longs to fill me, please enter my life with your fullness. I long to experience your closeness, but I also will not shun your silence; for you are faithful to continue your work in both. May I be faithful in return, and may my prayer to you always be 'Whatever, Lord.' Amen."

PUT AWAY YOUR COUPONS

Luci Swindoll

Woe . . . to those who say,
"Let God hurry, let him hasten
his work so we may see it.
Let it approach, let the plan
of the Holy One of Israel come,
so we may know it."

ISAIAH 5:18–19

I have just returned from lunch with Marilyn. We went to our favorite Mexican restaurant in the neighborhood. She wanted a potato taco, and I had the coupon that offers a second meal free. I figured that would be my meal. However, when all was said and done, Marilyn asked me for half the price of her meal, so I had to fork it over.

Don't you just love coupons? I do. In fact, when I got home from lunch and checked my mailbox, there was another bunch. I went through them hastily to see where I might want to go for dinner. To my delight they offered much more than meals. In fact, I figured I could start using them the next morning and keep myself busy all day.

I could start out with bacon and eggs for breakfast at Le Peep followed by a thigh-lift at The Plastic Surgery Institute. After a sandwich and bowl of soup at Donati's Grill, I could have my dog groomed at Pet Luv (the deal included a free goldfish — figure that out!) and get a haircut at Family Hair Salon. After relishing a pepperoni-with-double-cheese "Round Table" pizza for dinner, I could top off the day by being cremated at sundown for only $545. (I'm not kidding, there was a coupon I could fill out to get a free brochure on the Cremation Services of the Desert.)

In one little envelope was everything essential for the well-equipped woman. The gamut of choices reminds me of a little sign I once received from Barbara: "Eat well, Stay fit, Die anyway!"

On occasion I go to God's Word in search of a "coupon" — something I can tear out and take with me to use for a quick, half-price repair job. I don't really want it to cost me much, but I do want it to provide whatever I need for meeting the demands of that day. I don't have time to linger over the Scripture, so I say, "Lord, give me the short version, the coupon, the easy fix. After all, I've got things to do!" In short, I want God to hurry. But the Bible says woe to those who say, "Let God hurry." He doesn't take shortcuts.

Coupons save time and money. They provide immediate results and less expensive ways to have what we want or need. That's nice. But you know what? In God's economy there are no coupons or discounts. And do you know why? Because we don't need them. Discounts are unnecessary. The apostle Peter tells us, "His divine power has given us everything we need for life and godliness through our knowledge of him who called us by his own glory and goodness" (2 Peter 1:3).

Imagine! He has given us *everything* we need.

Unfortunately, most of us go through life feeling like we're long on need and short on resources. So we look for coupons. We present various offerings to the Lord as if he were some grocery-store clerk: "God, if you'll ____, I'll ____." We offer "coupons" to him and hope he'll redeem them. In the process, we miss the essence of what Peter taught. He assures us that, in Christ, and through his goodness, you and I have everything we need for life. When Christ redeemed us, he made coupon redemption superfluous.

Are you feeling long on need and short on resources today? Let me encourage you to do what I do when I feel that way: go to the One who has promised to provide everything you need, in abundance. He may not give you the answer you had envisioned, but you can trust it to be the perfect provision. He has promised his fullness. No half remedies. No special deals. So put away your coupons.

"Lord Jesus, you know what I need today, even better than I do. You know the longing of my soul and my deepest desire. Only you can fill that need because you know best. Thank you for promising to fill me with everything I truly need. I rest in you and what you will soon provide. Amen."

MINE!

Marilyn Meberg

Good will come to him who is
generous and lends freely,
who conducts his affairs with justice.

PSALM 112:5

I hope you don't mind just one more little Ian story. If you do, you can always flip on to read what eloquent things Patsy has to say . . . I'll never know. That's the great thing about a book. You could throw it down in a huff if you felt like it and no one would be offended.

At any rate, Ian had picked up a phrase that neither Beth nor Steve had taught him, so it came as a surprise when he started saying "no way" instead of his customary "no" when he wished to express a negative response. I thought it was a deliciously fun way to express resistance, and I started saying it along with him.

What intrigued me about his phrase was the way he said it. He had no anger or belligerence in his voice; it was always said with a quiet but plaintive tone as if he assumed his protest would go unheeded if he didn't make himself perfectly clear.

The morning that Beth, Ian, and I went to see Dr. Walker was one of those priceless times when his little "no way" protest took everyone off guard. Beth had been experiencing a nagging cough that had persisted since the beginning of her pregnancy, so in addition to the two-month pregnancy checkup, Dr. Walker's advice about the cough was solicited.

Beth was sitting on the exam table with Ian perched uncertainly on her lap. He wasn't sure what was going to go on in that room but whatever it was, it was obvious he didn't have peace about it. His little face was puckered in pensive disapproval as Beth described her cough, how long she'd had it, and so on. Dr. Walker put his stethoscope against her back and told her to take several deep breaths. Then he moved the stethoscope from her back and slipped it down the front of her blouse. That was too much for Ian. With startling clarity he pronounced "No way" and tried to push Dr. Walker's hand away. The doctor was stunned by these words from the baby he had delivered just seventeen months before. Chuckling, he said, "Getting too close to your milk supply, aren't I, little guy?"

Beth suggested I take Ian outside since it was only going to get worse. He wouldn't leave the room with me until Dr. Walker pretended to leave first.

As Ian and I repeatedly marched up and down the twenty-four steps outside the medical building, I thought about how the need to relinquish is a relentless part of daily living. Here's this tiny little fellow already faced with the need to relinquish his mama to some brutish doctor back in "that room." And in another seven months there will be more relinquishing when his baby sister arrives and takes over the house as well as the milk supply.

Our relinquishing may be as benign as giving up a parking spot to the person who feels certain she got there first. Or it may appear more crucially in our relationships: possibly a husband who seems to spend more time with the job than the family. It may well be that these priorities need to be examined, but it may also be good to consider how balanced we are in our expectations of each other's work time. Maybe we need to relinquish our inordinate need to have a spouse or a particular friend constantly at our side, listening to us, doing for us, and providing security for us. Or maybe we have parents who, now that they've retired, seem always to be off somewhere on a cruise or involved in some other activity that prevents them from being as available to us as we'd like. Perhaps we need to relinquish them to their hard-won freedom from the responsibilities they've carried all their lives.

Then of course there's that really tough one called relinquishing the children. Relinquishing them to marry someone we wouldn't choose, or to live too far away for frequent visits. Perhaps a son or daughter wants to attend a college or university that isn't our first choice. Do we need to relinquish our power and control and encourage them in their own choices?

Often we grasp too tightly whatever is a source of security for us. That usually indicates some early deprivation in our background, and we'd be wise to take a look at that and see if we're trying to get others to meet our needs. It's not the job of others to do that, unless of course we're seventeen months old and lunch appears to be in jeopardy.

What are you holding too tightly? What can't you relinquish, thinking that your next meal depends on it? Perhaps you and the

Lord could make that a prayer project with your ultimate goal being the ability to say, "Whatever, Lord."

"Lord Jesus, you remind us that you honor a generous heart and one that lends freely. May we learn to give more and demand less. Enable us to do more letting go and less holding on. May we simply yield to your sweet spirit of generosity and in so doing relinquish that part of us that fears not being in control. Take the reins from our grasping grip and teach us to rest in that release. Amen."

ONE OF A KIND

Being Yourself

YEP, THAT'S ME!

Patsy Clairmont

"The LORD does not look at the
things man looks at. Man looks at
the outward appearance,
but the LORD looks at the heart."

1 SAMUEL 16:7

I dashed into the local market, picked up some milk, bread, and a few goodies, and then made my way to the express checkout. The cashier looked at me and asked, "Now, don't you get a discount today?"

"No," I mumbled, wondering what she meant. She rang up my items while I puzzled over her query. I had glanced through our town newspaper earlier, and I couldn't recollect seeing any coupons. Maybe she thought I worked there and qualified for a discount.

Then suddenly it hit me like a ton of face cream: She thought I was a senior.

"Excuse me, but how would one qualify

for the discount?" I asked in a syrupy tone of voice.

She looked up and sweetly replied, "Oh, this is senior citizens' day for those over sixty."

That she could even consider me more than sixty years of age when I'm a mere fifty-one was disheartening. Not a news flash, just another older-than-you-look affirmation. If I had saved every old-age comment made to me through the years and if they were as valuable as, say, old comic books, I'd be sippin' soda under a palm tree on my own island.

I really believe we are a people hung up on our hormones and hairdos, but c'mon girls, none of us wants to wither before her time. Actually, I think this ancient countenance of mine is my grandmother's fault; she always looked centuries older than she was. When I was a child I was certain only Methuselah was older than my grandma. Yet she lived on for decades, bless her orthopedic heart.

Do you think, if we could get past our looks, we would be deeper people? I admit I like to look good. I take delight in developing a pleasing wardrobe. I enjoy compliments on my appearance. Yet even more meaningful is when someone tells me she enjoys my work. Or that the Lord has used me to open her eyes in some area of her life and encouraged her growth. Or that I brought her a smile in the midst of hard times. In fact, those kinds of comments actually make me feel . . . well . . . pretty.

I've also noticed that when I feel good about myself I seem to get more compliments about how I look. Do you think the condition of our heart and mind-set impacts our looks? I'm certain attitudes do.

I saw a young woman the other day who was wearing her 'tude like a tunic. She was wrapped up in herself and was looking for someone to vent on. I'm almost certain if she had dropped her attitude she would have been quite attractive, but what was visible was an angry, hostile countenance.

One way to defuse hostility is to accept ourselves. There is nothing more churning than to be in a constant tirade with the mirror. Not only does it discourage us, but it also sets us up for jealousy toward others, which adds to our anger. When we lighten up and learn to accept — and even appreciate — our looks, it relieves inner tension and others find us more attractive as well. Acceptance is a great way to achieve a face-lift.

Speaking of needing a face-lift . . . Think of the worst picture you have ever had taken of you. Now imagine someone enlarging it and sending it out to thousands of people without your knowledge. How would you feel?

I can tell you how I felt because that happened to me. I was surprised, hurt, embarrassed — and then I got over it. My husband often tells me when things don't go well: "Worse things happen in better families." In other words, *Don't sweat the small stuff.* Besides, even though it was a poor picture, when I saw it I had to admit, "Yep, that's me!"

Our looks are important because they are part of our uniqueness. They are proof we are one of a kind. So we need to appreciate our appearance but not idolize it. In the end, it won't be how we looked but how we loved that will matter.

"Lord, today as I fuss over my hair, my makeup, my clothes, help me to remember the makeover you started in me when we first became acquainted. And remind me to be willing to submit to any reworking you wish to undertake now. Amen."

To Bean or Not to Bean

Marilyn Meberg

Know that the LORD is God.
It is he who made us, and we are his.

PSALM 100:3

When Beth and Steve decided to get married in Italy, I realized I would need a coat! This southern California damsel did not even own a winter coat because I rarely needed one. But, I reasoned, if we were all going to traipse to Europe in the dead of winter, do the tourist thing by going to Paris first, and then do the wedding thing, I needed to ward off the potential of freezing to death.

L.L. Bean is a mail-order house in Freeport, Maine, whose catalogs I pore over regularly. I love that place! Almost all of my wool-cashmere blazers have come from there and my turtlenecks and sweaters as well. There's something irresistibly fun about simply picking up the phone, calling the toll-free number, and chatting with one of their amiable sales persons as I give my order. I always find out how cold it is there and then of course point out that we in southern California are basking in seventy-degree sunshine. (That's an unattractive side of me I'm not proud of, but I seem to continue to express it in spite of my disapproval.)

What better place to buy a warm coat for Europe than L.L. Bean! I was tremendously rushed that fall anyway and the ease of simply ordering my coat without leaving home was wonderful.

When my bright blue quilted goose-down long coat with optional zippered hood arrived, I felt ready for any temperature. It claimed to be lightweight for packing as well as wearing, and indeed it was. In fact, it proved to so efficiently retain my body heat, I never once felt cold in spite of freezing temperatures in Paris. I basically just cooed and smiled from the depths of my goose-down cocoon the entire three days we "did" Paris prior to going on to Italy.

Since then, this coat has cuddled and cocooned me many times: sitting on cold bleachers waiting for the Rose Bowl Parade to start, traveling to other cities whose temperatures nearly rival those of wintertime Paris, and then again just last week when we all went to New York for Thanksgiving. (I'd have died without her encompassing warmth while standing rinkside at Rockefeller Center.)

Perhaps now that I have so drawn you into my inordinate affection as well as appreciation of "Bean," you can possibly understand how startled I was to suddenly realize one morning as we all walked down West 75th to Amsterdam Street that no one in New York was wearing a bright blue quilted goosedown coat except me. Everyone was wearing a long black, brown, or tan wool coat. On the heels of this realization came a delayed flashback. I thought, *I don't remember anyone in Paris wearing a bright blue Bean either.*

I caught my reflection in a window as we hunched our way down Amsterdam to Sarabeth's for breakfast. *You know, Marilyn, you really look like a walking sleeping bag. I hate to tell you that, but you stick out in a crowd. There are no other walking sleeping bags in all of New York!* I was crushed.

After we'd given our breakfast order I turned to my son and said, "Jeff, I want your absolute, honest response. Do you like my coat?"

Jeff stared at me for a minute and then eyeballed the crush of not only my coat but the coats of Pat and Carla on the seat beside me. He said, "You mean the Bean?"

"Yeah . . . the Bean."

"Well, Mom, because of your happy attachment to her in Paris, I really care only that you continue to be pleased with her."

I looked closely at him to be sure he wasn't doing that Ken Meberg thing. "Jeff, what do you think of my Bean?"

"Mom, um . . . she's great for certain places and occasions."

"Jeff, is she good for New York?"

"Probably not, Mom."

"Jeff, was she good for Paris?"

"She kept you warm . . . but otherwise no, Mom — she belongs somewhere else."

I looked at my gorgeous fashion-plate daughter-in-law and said nothing. She too had the grace to say nothing.

My dear friend Pat whose fidelity to truth-telling is often a challenge to me offered, "I can tell you the exact place where Bean is appropriate."

Perking up I asked, "Where?"

"She would be appropriate for you to wear for duck hunting. You know . . . those places where people lie low and then rise up from the marshes with guns pointed and shoot at ducks who suddenly fly out of no-where."

I stared at her in total disbelief. "Pat, that's a terrible image. I can't imagine ever lying low to shoot a duck."

"Well, if you change your mind, you've got the coat for it!"

Fortunately our food arrived and I settled into my Florentine omelette with extra-crisp bacon on the side. The subject of my Bean didn't come up again.

I must admit there was a slight decrease in my usual ebullience as we went about our activities following breakfast. I was busy settling the Bean issue. So what if I were the only walking bright blue quilted person in New York . . . or Paris . . . or Amboy for that matter! Why do I have to mirror everyone else's subdued earth-tone wool look? I don't! I love my Bean . . . I'm cozy and warm in my Bean . . . and as Jeff pointed out, "We can always find you in a crowd!"

What more could one ask from a coat? That settled it: there would be no severing of my relationship with Bean. She stays, and so do I. Nestled beneath several layers of lightweight goose down I continued our New York activities, secure in the knowledge that I was the only genuinely warm person in the entire city!

Isn't it remarkable how uncomfortable we can become if we don't blend into our environment? But without God-given uniqueness, everything would look the same, taste the same, and feel the same. What a bore! And what a loss.

"May we learn, Lord Jesus, how dearly you love uniqueness and variety. Thank you that we all have different preferences and that there is no one quite like us on the earth. May we be pleased with our individuality, as you are pleased. Amen."

Stop Comparing

Luci Swindoll

> We do not dare to classify or compare ourselves with some who commend themselves. When they measure themselves by themselves and compare themselves with themselves, they are not wise.
>
> 2 Corinthians 10:12

The story of my life can be summed up in three words: *Bookended by Brilliance.*

Growing up in my family had a built-in challenge. My two brothers, by anybody's standards, are exceptional. They were as children, and they are now as adults. Both my older brother, Orville, and my younger brother, Chuck, are extremely accomplished, talented, musical, witty, warm, and loving. My challenge was to believe it was okay to be me without comparing myself to them. No one needed to tell me they were going to be "great" someday; I could sense it even in childhood.

Orville was always in a league of his own. He had his own ideas and dreams. Because he made top-notch grades, Mother and Daddy permitted him to have more privileges at a young age than other parents might have let their own sons have. Orville was an accomplished pianist, a math whiz, and a scholar. Not only that, but he was also an obedient son and attentive brother. He wasn't perfect, of course, but pretty close. My problem was that I wanted to be just like him.

Chuck, while quite different from Orville in temperament, was equally gifted and outstanding. Coupled with academic gifts was (and is) a tremendous sense of humor. He loves to laugh and has the ability to make everybody else laugh as well. Chuck and I were great pals as children, often pitting ourselves against the king of our immediate universe, Orville. We stood by each other and defended one another from Orville's lofty ambitions for which he wanted to engage us as slaves. Again, my problem was that I wanted to be just like Chuck.

Looking back now from fifty-plus years out, the saving grace in our family was that on the deepest level each of the siblings liked each other. We were proud of each other. And our parents didn't compare us to each other. They were far more interested in the development of our character than in our appearance or performance. In fact, if I remember correctly, our parents focused on where we were, who we were with, what we did, when we got home, and how we behaved. They emphasized learning, patriotism, family loyalty, and faith, and I believe they really sought to strike a balance in our home.

Even so, I compared myself with my brothers. Why? I don't know. No one had to spend time teaching me that; I managed it quite well on my own. It seems to be part of human proclivity, does it not? I've heard Chuck say numerous times in sermons: "Know yourself, like yourself, be yourself." For a great part of my life I've had to work toward the truth that it's *okay* to be me.

When Scripture teaches that it is not wise to measure or compare ourselves with others, I think we should pay attention. When we compare, we almost always come up short. Or, perhaps worse, we decide we're better than someone else. Either way, it causes stress.

If you're not happy with who you are, you'll spend precious energy trying to be somebody you're not, and it will wear you out. Think for a moment. Is there anybody in your life you're comparing yourself to? A beautiful sister? An accomplished brother? A friend who never seems to have problems? A sports figure who excels with little effort? Well, may I say with all the love in the world: *Quit it.* That business of comparing is going to make you sick and unproductive, if it hasn't already. You are you. God made you, you. And you are exactly who he wants you to be. Don't be somebody's clone. That person you're trying to be may very well be trying to be you.

Let's just all relax and be *ourselves*. It's so much easier. And a lot more fun.

"Lord, what a wonderful feeling it is that I don't have to be someone else . . . and they don't have to be me. You have called us each to be ourselves. Help me find the joy today in being me. *Amen."*

CRACKED POTS AND TARNISHED VESSELS

Patsy Clairmont

But we have this treasure in
earthen vessels, that the surpassing
greatness of the power may be of
God and not from ourselves.

2 CORINTHIANS 4:7 (nasb)

I attended a gala occasion recently to which I
wore a dressy pants outfit with stylish heels.
My hair was fluffed, and my ears were
adorned with a new pair of dazzling earrings.
I felt spiffy . . . until I arrived at the event. I
was the only woman with slacks on, and I felt
awkward. After a considerable time I spotted
another gal in slacks, and I wondered if she
would want to sit with me and be best
friends. Soon several others arrived in similar
attire, and I no longer felt the need to bond.

Aren't we funny? We work hard to be orig-
inals and then fear our originality has made

us different. I enjoy being center stage unless it's under a critical spotlight. Like the time I spoke only to learn afterward that my slip was hanging in a southerly direction waving to the onlookers. Following the session, several hundred women alerted me so I could hike it up. Believe me, I wanted to take a hike . . . an exceedingly long one to another land. Despite today's fads I prefer to keep my underwear undercover. Know what I mean?

Even though this blooper was embarrassing, I have lived long enough to understand that none of us has a corner on blunders. We are not one of a kind when it comes to gumming up the works; that's a human condition we all share. But we are exclusive in our mix of personalities, backgrounds, relationships, callings, and life choices. This means we are both like and unlike others.

I've noticed the people who seem most at home with themselves are not rocked by their faux pas. They are able to move past their flub-ups without remaining devastated or absorbing them into their sense of worth. I admire that since I used to be Ms. Flip-Out. The more I flitted and fought against my humanity the more flubs I seemed to make and the worse I felt. I was emotionally in a stir. Gradually I gave up my attempts to be something I wasn't (perfect), which made it possible for me to be more comfortable with who I am (a one-of-a-kind cracked pot).

Of course, some days I fall back into old patterns. Then I have to be reminded by other flawed, yet one-of-a kind vessels of my freedom in Christ.

Speaking of flawed, I guess we could say Jonah the prophet was a fishy vessel. His calling was to be a landlubber, but instead he headed for the deep blue sea. Jonah sprung a leak and sunk in over his head before he realized his error and finally agreed to fulfill his one-of-a-kind calling by high-stepping it over to Nineveh to stand alone.

It's not easy to stand alone, and it certainly is a test of our willingness to be a one-of-a-kind-er. Ask Eve. She was an earthen vessel in the truest form, a one-and-only woman if ever there was one. Unable or unwilling to resist the enemy's fruity fling, she lost the sweetness of her highest calling.

It would seem that standing alone would take stamina, determination, and discipline. Uh-oh, these aren't my majors. Unless you count willfulness. No, wait, that's what cost Eve Paradise. Even though Eve was unique, her sin made her common . . . as does ours.

Sin tarnishes our one-of-a-kind brilliance. I have a copper pot that quickly dulls when not tended to. It has to be cleaned and polished regularly. We also lose our individual luster and become no more than common pots when we are tainted by sinful behavior.

King David, a royal pot with a deadly plot, marred his regal rank when he went for a dish on the side. His sinful actions to steal another man's wife and murder her husband robbed him of his one-of-a-kind reputation. Sin is both costly and cheap.

I've observed men and women with powerful callings diminish their one-of-a-kind effectiveness by heading out in wrong directions, making poor choices, and wanting what isn't theirs. And here's the kicker: We are all susceptible to behaving commonly and missing our individual best. All we cracked pots and tarnished vessels need to heed the lessons of Jonah, Eve, and David, and strive toward keeping our individual containers shipshape.

"Dear Jesus, help us to be comfortable, not with sin, but with your one-of-a-kind design for us. We want to be our sparkling best, but

we will need your cleansing protection, for we are willful. Thank you for pursuing Jonah until he followed you; for allowing Eve to experience fruit from her womb rather than just the fruit of her sin; and for graciously receiving King David when he sought your forgiveness. This gives all of us tarnished pots hope. Amen."

TWO PLUS TWO EQUALS WHAT?

Marilyn Meberg

"Before I formed you
in the womb I knew you."

JEREMIAH 1:5

I believe the first soul-thud recognition of my enormous math deficit hit me at the age of ten. I had been placed in an accelerated math class by a teacher who erroneously assumed I belonged there. I suppose that assumption was based upon the fact that I was doing fine in accelerated reading and writing classes.

I was vaguely aware that the fog rolled in whenever I caught sight of a number, but in that advanced class the density of the fog was so great I couldn't even make out who was sitting in front of me. My pitiful performance soon caught the attention of the teacher and I was "decelerated" to a class of other fog-enshrouded children.

Though this was a relief to me in that the pressure to perform was lessened, from that point on I began to question my own adequacy. Thoughts like "teachers think you're smart but then they find out you're not" loomed in my mind. I wondered how I could be so comfortable with words and so dense with numbers. Something, I assumed, was obviously wrong with my brain.

As I grew older and my dismal performance with numbers endured, I compensated by avoiding them as much as possible. By the time I entered college I felt relieved that math could go its way and I would go the opposite. I got a B.A. degree in English and to my knowledge never encountered a number the entire four years!

When our son Jeff was about two years old, I was a bit restless and felt the need for stimulation beyond high chairs, sandboxes, and tot trikes. Ken suggested I enroll in the graduate program at California State University located in our town of Fullerton, and begin a master's degree in English. The idea was to take just one class each semester (one night a week) until I finished. There was no rush; I was just there for fun. What a great idea!

I soon learned, however, that there was a major challenge to be faced along with this aspiration: it was called the Graduate

Record Exam. Not only would I be tested in those areas in which I had always excelled, but my math skills (or lack of them) would be tested as well.

I well remember sitting in a hot stuffy room, staring dumbfounded at pages and pages of math questions. Predictably, the fog came rolling in. "Now wait a minute, Marilyn . . . don't give into the old feeling of inadequacy. What you need to do is not bother reading the questions; they only confuse you. Since you merely have to black in either A, B, C, or D for each answer, simply construct a pattern. Mark a few A's, zip over to a few D's, balance the design with some scattered B's and C's, and see if you like the look of it. If not, change the pattern entirely: do all A's, then all B's, and skip D's altogether!" That plan lifted my spirits enormously and I got right to work on a pleasing pattern.

When the computerized results were mailed to our house weeks later, I of course couldn't make sense of the various percentages, but as Ken was interpreting them for me he began to laugh almost uncontrollably when he got to the math results. "Marilyn, there are actually three percent of the graduate population who scored lower in math than you did!"

"Really . . ." I said with mounting confidence. "You mean there are actually people who took that math part who did more poorly than I?"

"Absolutely, Marilyn . . . good for you!"

I pondered that happy news for a few minutes and then asserted with genuine compassion, "Those people should never have read the questions. That's probably why they didn't do as well as I did."

It has taken me some time to come to terms with the fact that I simply do not, never did, and never will feel comfortable in the presence of a number. However, for years I longed to be like everyone else in the world whom, I perceived, could add a column of numbers so quickly that drool gathered in the corners of my mouth as I watched.

I simply do not have a numerical gift. I do, however, provide endless merriment for my friends as I valiantly try to calculate the tip from a lunch tab or stare blankly at the dinner table wondering why there are only five place settings while six people are waiting to be seated. I am as consistent in my deficit as Los Angeles smog. People can count on me. I have finally embraced my deficit with a reluctant warmth. After all, there's something to be said for consistent inability: It makes others feel secure.

♥

"Lord Jesus, I am who I am by your loving design. Help me to accept my weaknesses as well as my strengths. Help me, too, to embrace myself in my totality as you embrace me, knowing I cannot do what was not ordained for me. May I contentedly serve you, love you, and luxuriate in what you empower me to do in your name and for your sake. Amen."

YOU'RE A STAR!

Barbara Johnson

"Those who are wise will shine
like the brightness of the heavens,
and those who lead many to
righteousness, like the stars
for ever and ever."

DANIEL 12:3

Have you noticed how Americans have gone star struck? Our appetite to know more about the lives of the rich and famous seems to be insatiable. We are obsessed with faces of movie stars and inquiry into their private lives. Talk shows, news programs, women's and even news magazines seem to be moving further from true journalism and more toward fluff about the famous.

What's happening to us, anyway? Have we given up *real* life in order to take on *reel* life? It seems like we all wish we were stars.

Did you ever wonder what it would be like to be one? Well, you are! You are God's

215

kingdom star. You may be overweight, sport age spots, find a new crinkle in your face now and then. None of that matters. For your beauty is generated from the inside. Stars don't merely reflect the light of the sun like the moon does. Stars *are* little suns; they generate their own light.

When my boys were small we bought some decals in the shape of stars and constellations to put on the ceiling of their bedroom. When the lights were turned off, the decals glowed in the darkness, making the ceiling luminous and sparkly. When the boys' friends came over to spend the night, they enjoyed bedtime. They'd run to turn off the light and then just lie beneath the blankets enjoying the nighttime sky. The magic of starlight captured their imagination.

I thought of that recently when we were visiting our youngest son, Barney, who lives in the country. The stars in the rural Nevada skies were brighter than anything we used to see in Los Angeles where the boys grew up. Barney remembered the glittery decals from his room and is happy to be raising his children where they see the real thing.

How many stars are there? Astronomers don't know. They assure us the cosmos contains more stars than can be counted. Did you ever think about how a new star is created? In physics, nuclear fusion occurs when two separate elements are forced together. Through extreme pressure and temperature, a surge of energy is suddenly released. The elements are transformed into something entirely new. A star!

In this dark world, our material life and spiritual life are forced together under the pressure of trials and troubles — the hotter, the more explosive. Energy is released in the power of the Holy Spirit and a brand new being is created. We are transformed into a bright force, giving off light and warmth. Our testimony may mean that someone, somewhere will find her way home. Someone will stop to wonder about God. Someone with a heavy load will take comfort in the starlight.

But there is more. It's like this: A little child was walking one evening with his mother. He looked up at the sky and said, "Mommy, if the wrong side of heaven is this beautiful, imagine what the right side looks like!"

Maybe we don't appear to amount to much. But imagine how we'll look when we're turned right side out!

The psalmist exhorted the stars to praise God. I think he was thinking of the topside of heaven. When we get there, all our questions will be answered because there will be no shadows, no dark corners, no place to hide from the light. In heaven, we'll realize the true brilliance and beauty of our lives.

Though you may feel like insignificant stardust here on earth, remember: you're a star. Live like one!

"Dear Lord Jesus, you stood with your Father and with him created light on this earth. But it is a mere speck of the light in your own home. We know someday we will live with you in perfect knowing. Everything will be clear. There will be no more sighing or sobbing. But today, help us shine like the stars we are, for as long as someone needs us. Amen."

No Strings Attached

Barbara Johnson

But the fruit of the Spirit is love, joy, peace, patience, kindness, goodness, faithfulness, gentleness and self-control.

GALATIANS 5:22–23

The little boy had just moved into a new neighborhood. His name was Brad, and he was very quiet and shy. One February day when he got home from school he told his mom he knew Valentine's Day was coming up and he wanted to make a valentine for every child in his class.

Brad's mom's heart sank. She was certain her little boy's heart would be hurt in the process of giving, because every afternoon she watched all the kids walking home from school, laughing and hanging onto each other — all except Brad. He trudged along behind them.

But she went along with his idea and bought him some red and white paper, glue, crayons, and glitter. Day after day Brad spent his after-school hours painstakingly creating thirty-five one-of-a-kind valentines.

When the day came to deliver them, he was so excited. With the precious bundle under his arm, he raced out the door early to get to school before all his classmates arrived. His mother thought sadly, *This will be such a tough day for Brad. I'm going to bake him some of his favorite cookies and have them warm and ready for him when he gets home. I wish I could do more to ease the pain he'll feel when he doesn't get very many valentines.*

That afternoon she put the warm cookies and milk on the table and went to the window to watch for her son. Sure enough, here came the big gang of children, laughing, bright valentines under their arms. And there was Brad, trailing behind. He was walking faster than usual and she thought, *Bless his heart, his arms are empty and he's about to burst into tears.*

When he came into the house she said tenderly, "Honey, Mommy has some warm cookies and milk for you." She was startled to see that his face was aglow. He just marched past her as he declared triumphantly: "I didn't forget a single one . . . not a single one!" He was grinning from ear to ear.

What a message for those of us who forget that the greatest joy is not in receiving, but in giving from our one-of-a-kind hearts. When we get outside ourselves enough to let God's life flow through us, the sweet fruit of his Spirit will grow and nourish everyone around us.

Do you have spiritual fruit in your life today? What are you doing to actively show love and kindness to other people in the humble spirit of Christ? If you have been caught up in what you are — or are not — getting from others, think about little Brad. Then ask God how he wants to use your one-of-a-kind self to touch someone today. Give his love away with joy in your heart. No strings attached.

"Lord Jesus, remind me continually that your love seeks nothing for itself but gives generously out of its abundance. Because you love me, I always have enough love to give away to anyone who crosses my path. Let me experience the joy of giving in your name. Amen."

EPITAPHS

Luci Swindoll

Give her the reward she
has earned, and let her works
bring her praise at the city gate.

PROVERBS 31:31

As an art major in college, I often painted outdoors. Laden with easel, paints, brushes, water can, and camp stool I would strike out to wherever the flowers were prettiest. More often than not that led me to the local cemetery. It was delightful being outside in the sunshine, and I was always intrigued with the headstones on various graves: the bas relief carved in cement, the words that supposedly reflected the person whose bones rested there. To me it was all very fascinating.

As the semester progressed I found I was as interested in the epitaphs on the tombstones as I was in the flowers that bloomed throughout the cemetery. I stooped down to read many of them and found it remarkable that a few short words could sometimes capture the entire essence of a person.

It is my understanding that W. C. Fields, for example, has etched on his tombstone, "On the whole, I'd rather be in Philadelphia." And how about the woman who had her potato salad recipe carved into her headstone. Apparently, during her lifetime everybody wanted that recipe and her response was always: *Over my dead body.* I have a close friend who never gets quite as much sympathy as she likes when she's feeling bad, so she wants to be remembered by these loving words: *See, I told you I was sick.*

Most of us won't have the prerogative to write our own epitaph. It will be written by someone else . . . someone who will seek to capture a single phrase epitomizing our entire life. If you were to die today, what phrase captures your essence? What words characterize you?

In a sense, we are writing our epitaph everyday. What would yours say today? I know people who are so rich in character that there are not enough words in the English language to describe the beauty and outreach of their life, much less to reduce that life to a single phrase. On the other hand, I know folks whose cantankerous spirit leaves one searching for something . . . anything . . . that can summarize their life kindly.

For some of us, the message on our tombstone seems like something in the far-distant future. However, we never know. (Reminds me of a friend who told me she's used up so many sick days, she's going to have to phone in *dead*.) James 4:14 tells us, "Why, you do not even know what will happen tomorrow. What is your life? You are a mist that appears for a little while and then vanishes."

Picture that in your mind's eye. A vanishing vapor, *poof!* What could be more uncertain?

The Creator has made us each one of a kind. There is nobody else exactly like us, and there never will be. Each of us is his special creation and is alive for a distinctive purpose. Because of this, the person we are, and the contribution we make by being that very person, are vitally important to God.

That makes me want to be *today* exactly who God made me, and no one else. This may be the last day I have.

"Father, thank you that you designed me uniquely. You've gifted me uniquely, and you have a unique plan for me. Show me that plan today, and give me the grace and courage to live it out with gusto. Amen."

THE GREATEST "JOY BREAK"

Marilyn Meberg

"And what a difference between
man's sin and God's forgiveness!"

ROMANS 5:15 (tlb)

Our first home was one that pleased Ken and
me enormously. We loved our little fenced-in
backyard and felt confident about the safety
of both Jeff and Beth as they trundled about
in it, often without need of our direct super-
vision.

On either side of the walkway leading to
the front door was an area of decorative
small rocks. Jeff loved to play in there with
his Tonka trucks, creating roads and garages
for his fleet of vehicles. Ken had attempted
to impress upon Jeff's four-year-old mind
the importance of keeping the rocks out of
the grass because of the damage it would do
to his lawnmower. In fact, Ken explained to

Jeff that he was solely responsible for keeping the grass clear of rocks even if it were his friends and not Jeff who, in a burst of driving frenzy, managed to spew rocks into the grass.

One Friday morning as Jeff and I were bringing groceries into the house I noticed some rocks were strewn about the grass area near the front door. I suggested to Jeff that he would need to get out there and remove them since Daddy would be mowing the next day. Jeff was indignant at the suggestion. "I didn't get those rocks in there . . . Nell did!"

"It doesn't matter who got them there, sweetheart. It's your job to keep the grass clear. That's Daddy's deal with you."

"That's not right . . . I didn't do it."

"I'm sorry, Jeff, but you still need to clear the grass whether it feels fair to you or not."

Jeff was always a mild-mannered little fellow and not the least prone to fits and fights. He trudged resolutely outside but from his body language I could see he was laboring under a burden of victimization.

The kitchen window was open and I could hear him muttering to himself as he sifted through the grass removing rocks. I was enormously curious to know the contents of his muttering so I leaned in the direction of the window. "I'm just like Jesus ... I'm just like Jesus ... I'm just like Jesus."

That was the last thing I expected to hear. What in the world was going on in his little mind? I decided to go outside and help him with the rock detail and while there, ask him if he would talk about how he was just like Jesus. At first he would neither mutter nor talk to me. Finally, with my prodding, he retorted, "Well, Jesus never did anything bad and he got punished. That's just the same as me!"

I enveloped his troubled little face with my eyes and then swooped him into my arms. He didn't cry but I did.

Jeff's theology was a bit off, but we didn't go into it then. It is true that Jesus "who knew no sin" died that I, born in sin, might have eternal life. That is a difficult truth to comprehend at times. I love the clarity with which The Living Bible expresses this in Romans 5:15–17: "For this one man, Adam, brought death to many through his sin. But this one man, Jesus Christ, brought forgiveness to many through God's mercy. Adam's one sin brought the penalty of death to many, while Christ freely takes away many sins and gives glorious life instead. The sin of this one man, Adam, caused death to be king over all, but all who will take God's gift of forgiveness and acquittal are kings of life because of this one man, Jesus Christ."

Some years later, these regenerating truths became more clear to Jeff. Ultimately he came to understand that we not only identify with the sufferings of Christ, but we are set free because of the sufferings of Christ. What colossal good news!

As you are reading this book and contemplating the Jesus about whom we speak, I pray that you too know him personally. Without that precious relationship it is impossible to know the greatest "joy break" of all.

"Lord Jesus, you who set us free from all the sin and condemnation that came upon the world through disobedience, we thank you. We thank you for our salvation; we thank you for our freedom; we thank you that there is no condemnation to those who are in Christ Jesus. We thank you that our acceptance of you as Savior means we are securely held in your embrace now and forever. Amen."

DOT TO DOT

Connecting to Sisterhood

CONNECTED

Patsy Clairmont

You are no longer foreigners and aliens,
but fellow citizens with God's people
and members of God's household.

EPHESIANS 2:19

Have you ever noticed how the Lord connected people (Adam-Eve, David-Jonathan, Mary-Elizabeth)? And still does (Marilyn, Barbara, Luci, and me)? I love the dot-to-dot concept of people being involved with other people. I confess some dots are more my kind of dots than others. For instance, I'm drawn to exclamation points, like the "Joyful Journey" gals. Working and traveling with these dynamic dots is truly a joyous experience.

Since I live in Michigan and Luci, Marilyn, and Barbara live in California, staying connected with them takes some effort. We share sporadic phone calls and squeeze in mail whenever we can. Sometimes when I'm talking to Marilyn on the phone, she'll pass along information for me to Luci and Barbara, and vice-versa. Occasionally we have a conference call, which is a hoot. Picture four loquacious women all trying to say something vital at the same time.

Barbara has the gift of phone. Although not listed in the New Testament gifts (she has some of those, too), it's her delightful way to help us all stay connected. She calls frequently, full of giggles and fun. Barbara also has the gift of cheerleading. She roots us on, as well as many others throughout the land. If Barbara learns any of us has succeeded at anything, she is the first to offer accolades.

Marilyn and I have had a number of telephone talks that range from meaningful to medicinal to criminal (well, almost). We speak shorthand in an attempt to get in all our words, and our chats are riddled with laughter. The accumulation of conversations have kept Marilyn and me connected and have added to our growing friendship.

Luci is the world's greatest letter writer. Not that her letters are long, but they are works of art. If we could have a letter contest for design and creativity, Luci would win. Why, even her signature is a joy to behold, not to mention her witty sayings, her profound insights, and her off-the-chart humor.

We four also go out of our way to share jokes, cartoons, and funny happenings with each other because we know how intense life gets, and we need joy breaks. The girls (term of endearment) also sent me flowers when my book, *Sportin' a 'Tude*, was well received in the marketplace. I was touched to have them think of me and applaud my good fortune. There's nothing sweeter than to have friends who share in your joy.

Speaking of shared joy, remember when Mary, the soon-to-be mother of Jesus, visited the aging (and pregnant) Elizabeth? Even Elizabeth's unborn child leapt for joy when the women met (Luke 1:41). What a beautiful picture of celebrating another's blessings and connecting at deep levels in each other's lives. And to think they were relatives — that impresses me even more. Lots of us don't relate well to our relations.

Recently my cousin Ann, whom I had not heard from since we were children, contacted me. What a surprise, and how tickled I was to learn she wanted to reconnect after all these years. (We were raised in different states, and our life journeys never had occasion to intersect.) Ann said she woke up one day and realized she had lost contact with her father's (my uncle's) family. Now in her sixties, she decided to call all of her first cousins and to reestablish relationships. I couldn't have been more pleased, and so we agreed to meet up at one of my conferences in the south. Our reunion was fun and allowed us to reestablish our family connection. Isn't that what connecting is really all about — being like family?

I was at the grocery store today when a learning-disabled friend of mine greeted me. After saying hello, he asked me, "Patsy, do you like me?"

"Yes, I do," I answered without hesitation. Satisfied with my answer, he went merrily on his way.

I guess if we were all that honest, we could get to the bottom line a lot faster in relationships. "Do you like me" kind of sums it up, doesn't it? We all long to know that we have the strong link of acceptance connecting us.

"Thank you, Lord Jesus, for the Calvary connection that makes us family. Amen."

A NUMBER-TEN FRIEND

Patsy Clairmont

A friend loves at all times.

PROVERBS 17:17

Friendship is a word full of growth potential. One can become bigger (as in character enlargement) or one can become smaller (as in narrow-minded). Becoming a good friend is aerobic in that it takes time and effort. We don't just wake up one day, and voila: we are Wonder Friend! The need for companionship is built into our genes, but we don't come with the know-how to be a comrade. That is learned through giving, taking, forgiving, sharing, praying, and empathizing.

Most of us feel we know what it takes to be a good friend. Yet, if that's true, why do we have so many lonely people who long for meaningful friendships? Perhaps too many of us are wanting someone to be our friend instead of being someone's friend ourselves. Also, it's easy to make mistakes in relationships. I know I've certainly flubbed up enough times. Maybe you feel that way, too. In fact, let's take a gander at "Twelve Ways to Insure a Small Repertoire of Friends":

1. Breed pettiness.
2. Campaign against your friend's mate.
3. Drop in frequently.
4. Offer unsolicited advice.
5. Create opportunities to whine.
6. Nitpick their children.
7. Besiege her with phone calls.
8. Critique her decisions.
9. Encourage dissension.
10. Share freely in all her possessions.
11. Snub her other friends.
12. Insist on being her best friend.

Any of those ring a bell? They are surefire ways to remain lonely.

So, what does it take to have healthy, warm relationships? Let's peer at what makes a priceless friend. We will call it, "Twelve Ways to Be a Number-Ten Friend."

1. Believe the best.
2. Respect and set boundaries.
3. Express humor to release joy (not venom).

4. Applaud successes.
5. Maintain good manners.
6. Draw a generous friendship circle.
7. Give without expectations.
8. Praise genuinely (no gushing).
9. Support her frailty (no indulging).
10. Protect private information.
11. Pray fervently.
12. Love Jesus passionately.

Remember to leave room in your friendships for failure; otherwise, when people let you down (which they will), you will have to replace them. How exhausting. Besides, I've learned some of my most revealing lessons about myself while working through conflict.

My feelings used to get hurt much more easily than they do today. What a relief to have greater resiliency. Also, I've learned that when I don't enter into my friends' successes with joy, it's usually because I'm jealous. Ouch, that's painful to confess . . . even to myself. Jealousy is like a spider's web. It's difficult to see its slender fibers, easy to get entangled in, and hard to brush off.

The last piece of friendship advice (to

love Jesus passionately) is the best counsel of all. When Jesus is our best friend, we won't approach human friendships from such a fragile place and turn people off by our consuming neediness. Jesus longs to be our Need Meeter. When we turn to him first and then turn to others, we will be better prepared to give and receive relationally and rationally.

Friendship is such an honor, our lives intersecting with others in meaningful ways. This makes friendship a joy break of the finest kind!

"Lord, let's do lunch, just the two of us . . . We'll talk. Amen."

HURTS CASTLE

Barbara Johnson

Unless the LORD builds the house,
its builders labor in vain.

PSALM 127:1

In the San Francisco Bay area there is a tourist attraction called the Winchester Mystery House. It was owned during the Victorian era by the heiress of the Winchester rifle company. Guilt-ridden and superstitious, this multimillionaire wanted to appease the spirits of people killed by her family's famous weapons. She determined to confound any ghosts that may come to haunt her home by continuously remodeling it. Builders worked nonstop creating rooms and hallways with bizarre configurations.

Among other mysterious things in this three-story house is a staircase leading nowhere, a labyrinth leading to the master bedroom, an exquisite Tiffany window facing a solid wall, and repetitious use of

239

patterns with thirteen components: thirteen window panes, tiles, and so forth. At one point she even had the magnificent front door entirely boarded up.

Like Ms. Winchester, each of us is in process of remodeling our life's mansions until the day we die. Ms. Winchester's mansion was a reflection of her disoriented inner life; as Christians, however, we are not motivated by fear. We work under the leading of the Holy Spirit. We plan, erect, shingle, illuminate, adorn, and furnish our lives with his anointing. We fill them with laughter, not superstition. We light them with love, not dim paranoia. We decorate them with encouraging words, not enigmatic phrases meant to trick evil spirits. And as for the front door, it is anointed with the precious blood of Jesus and open to God, friends, and strangers alike. Our lives are like exquisite homes where we create a haven of safety from the assaults of the world.

A friend of mine lives in an Oregon forest near the high desert. Winters can be hard, but there is plenty of juniper to burn, a wood that smells heavenly. My friend enjoys walks in the late afternoon when people stoke up their stoves for the evening and turn on lamps as darkness falls. The cozy smells from chimneys and the glow from neighborhood windows create a comforting atmosphere.

Sometimes I call my life's mansion "Hurts Castle." The light of hope shines on the front porch. Inside there is always a soft shoulder to cry on. I try to create the same feeling here I had as a little girl when I'd run home from school during blustery Michigan winters. I remember the crunch of snow under my galoshes as I ran up the steps. Inside, the tantalizing aroma of my mother's homemade soup enfolded me. I'd warm up by the heating grate in the floor, feeling the whoosh of warm air all around me.

In my mansion, the hearth is burning with enthusiasm and the light of God. Ruth Graham, wife of the evangelist, Billy, named one of her books *Come Sit by My Laughing Fire*. When I saw that title, I thought, *yes, that's it!* The laughing fire is one that sputters with joy while it burns away the troubles of the day.

God wants you to build a laughing fire on the hearth of your mansion. Use the fuel of his love to turn trouble into heat and energy for yourself and other people. Stoke the smoldering embers of your passion for life. As the smoke curls from the chimney, other people will be drawn to the sweet aroma of compassion.

In *Mere Christianity*, C. S. Lewis says to imagine God coming in to rebuild your house: "At first you understand what he is doing. Presently he starts knocking the house about in a way that doesn't seem to make sense . . . You thought you were going to be made into a decent little cottage, but He is building a palace. He intends to come and live in it Himself."

Is there an inviting glow and a heavenly scent to your life? Invite the Lord into it. He'll make it a place of divine mystery and glory that will provide safe haven for others as they pass by on their own journey toward him.

"Enlarge my heart (not my hips!), oh Lord. Bless my home — the one I am creating for other people through my personality and experience and attitude. I want this to be a happy place for others to rest a while and renew their strength. Thank you for your salvation through Jesus and the promise of a spectacular mansion in heaven. Amen."

Coloring the Night Away

Marilyn Meberg

But the rich have many friends.

Proverbs 14:20

Last night Pat and I had agreed to spend the evening together engaged in some wild and woolly activity yet to be determined. As we discussed various options I became increasingly aware of my fatigue from a very demanding week. From that fatigue came a most soothing, novel, and appealing idea.

I announced to Pat: "I want to buy crayons and a coloring book and spend the evening coloring." She stared at me for a minute trying to hide the look of incredulity on her face. Then, assuming her best therapist voice, she asked what kind of coloring book would please me and how many crayons I wanted. Pretending not to notice her clinical tone, I said I wanted at least twenty-four different colored crayons and that I would know the coloring book when I saw it.

With a kindly affirmation from Pat that spending the evening coloring might indeed be pleasant, she agreed to the plan. She did ask, however, if I thought smoking cigars while we colored would add a dimension of the adult to our activity. Since neither of us have the faintest notion of even how to smoke — much less a cigar — we quickly gave up that idea as not only impractical but unappealing as well.

True to expectation I found the perfect coloring book for me. It was called *The Huckleberry Finn Coloring Book. Huckleberry Finn* has always been one of my favorite novels, and I was instantly gratified by my purchase. Pat chose a coloring book of Disney characters which I thought was a bit beneath her level of sophistication, but I didn't think it would be kind to say so.

Armed with my new coloring book and a box of twenty-four crayons (Pat had to buy her own; I told her I absolutely would not share mine), I settled down to one of the most soothing and delightful evenings I've had in ages. While I determined the perfect color combination for the Widow Douglas's dress as well as the apron of her sister Miss Watson, we listened to Christmas music.

Even though it wasn't yet Thanksgiving, and in spite of feeling slightly confused, I enjoyed it enormously.

I think it only fair to report that I was ready to quit coloring long before Pat was. In fact, I suspect she took up her crayons again after I left for home that evening.

I love the fact that God is a God who encourages relationship not just with himself, but with each other. Jesus modeled that for us in the richness of his relationships with the twelve disciples. We are indeed rich when we have many friends, and I'm thoroughly convinced that God loves us, encourages us, nurtures us, and supports us through other human beings. They can almost become to us Jesus with skin.

May we not become so busy, harried, and overcommitted that we neglect that part of our soul that is fed and sustained by friendship.

"Lord Jesus, how grateful I am for other people in your great creation who can cradle my soul and hear my voice in much the same manner in which you cradle my soul and hear me. Thank you for bringing these ambassadors of your love into my world. Amen."

245

THE GREEKS HAVE STOLEN MY HEART

Luci Swindoll

"As you sent me into the world,
I have sent them into the world."

JOHN 17:18

Opposites attract, so they say. And I think they're right.

For more than twenty-five years I have been close friends with a Greek family who lives in Athens. From all outward experience, we have little in common. We don't think in the same language, live in the same country, share the same culture, or embrace the same political values. Perhaps most significantly, we do not have the same philosophy of life. Nevertheless, our friendship has grown and blossomed. That's because we've found common ground in matters of the heart. We love each other.

The first Stylianidou family member I

met was Sophia. Through her I met her older sister, Klea, Klea's husband, Achilles, and their daughter, Madelene. Sophia's parents, Panagiotis and Maria, became my friends as well. I was a tourist in Greece when I met them and have since returned eight times to be their house guest.

Because of the stark differences between us, the distance in miles, and the obvious work it took to keep this friendship alive, there were numerous times I could have given up. But I can honestly say that thought never crossed my mind. I can't imagine my life without my Greek friends in it. In fact, the challenge of keeping up to date has been a great part of the joy.

Through the years, we have wept, laughed, mourned, and danced together. Numerous friends of mine have met Sophia when they have visited Athens. With great intensity and enthusiasm we have maintained a system of letter writing and gift giving that has bonded us even more. But the most important thing we have enjoyed together is the conversation: face-to-face, by telephone, or in those letters. We've said it all!

During my most recent visit, Klea and I had one of our usual delightful conversations. She was wearing a rather large ring I was admiring which became translucent when held up to the light. Etched into it was the Greek god, Jupiter. The exchange went something like this:

K: "Lusaki, do you know Jupiter?"
L: "You mean the Greek god, Jupiter?"
K: "Yes."
L: "Well, yes, somewhat . . . but what about him?"
K: "He is the god who changed himself into other forms to do something he wanted to do. On this ring he has changed himself into rain . . . can you see it?" (She held it up to the light.)
L: "Oh yes, I see it . . . but why did he become rain?"
K: "Because he wanted to make love with Danae."
L: "Danae? Who is Danae?"
K: (With a flick of her wrist and a thoughtful look) "Oh, I don't know . . . some Greek godness."

I howled. Everything so serious and accurate till the end of the story; then, as though she tired of her own storytelling, "Oh, I don't know . . . some Greek godness." I *cracked up!*

On that same trip, Klea and I had several

conversations about the Lord. In fact, I walked through her door one day and the first thing she said was, "Lusaki, tell me everything you know about God." I couldn't tell her everything, but I had the opportunity to share the gospel. Little did I know that would be my last conversation with Klea. She died this year of breast cancer. Across the miles, Sophia and I have tried to comfort one another in our grief. This has been a profound loss.

One of my great concerns — something I see frequently in Christian circles — is the tendency to isolate ourselves from those who are different from us. We gravitate toward people who think like we think, agree with us on everything, believe like we do, even dress the same. In so doing we miss wonderful, God-given opportunities to expand our understanding of the world and the people in it.

Jesus prayed for us about this, specifically in John 17:15 and 18: "My prayer is not that you take them out of the world but that you protect them from the evil one. . . . As you sent me into the world, I have sent them into the world."

In this world, I wouldn't have wanted to miss the Stylianidou family . . . not one single member. Don't bypass the potential for meaningful relationships just because of differences. Explore them. Embrace them. Love them.

"You have left me in this world, Lord, because there are people here you love and to whom I can become your representative. Make me a loving ambassador for this divine mission. And thank you that it can be so much fun! Amen."

BE A JOY GERM

Barbara Johnson

Like cold water to a weary soul
is good news from a distant land.

PROVERBS 25:25

In my college there was a sweet tradition: Each evening about nine o'clock a young man would bring notes from guys to the girls' dormitory. A bell would ring and we girls would dash down to the lobby. The notes usually asked for a date or to sit with a favorite girl at a performance, or contained just a few affectionate words.

For some girls, this was a painful tradition because there were never notes for them. I remember one girl who was just a little "different." Her clothes never matched or fit right and she had difficulty speaking clearly. She stopped coming down or expecting anything. Then one night her name was called out. It happened several nights in a row, then at least once or twice a week. Each time

251

she received an anonymous note complimenting her on some special thing she did that was appreciated. The notes were like a gift straight from God to her.

This girl never did find out who sent her the notes, but the fellow who had written them became a good friend of mine and confided in me about it. He was sort of "different," too. He'd lost his hair due to a childhood disease and also had a speech impediment. But he had a gentle and sensitive spirit. He cared enough to let one individual know how special she was beyond what people saw on the outside. He changed her experience of herself that year.

When we do little acts of kindness that make life more bearable for someone else, we are walking in love as the Bible commands us. One way to do this costs only the sum of a postage stamp, a little paper and ink. Every one of us has felt the nudge to write someone a letter or note. Many times we don't follow up on it; we tell ourselves it wouldn't matter anyway. When we think this way, we miss giving and receiving splashes of joy.

I receive many notes from women who are hurting or burdened, yet care enough to let me know my ministry has meant something to them. I put their notes in my joy box, and when I need a special pick-me-up I sit down and read them all over again. Sometimes the salutation alone means as much as the message itself. Sometimes the beauty of the card inspires me. Or the handwriting is full of emotion, or there are cute stickers that make me smile.

Someone you know is crossing a desert in her life and can use a drink of cold water. Will you be the one to bring it to her? Take up your pen! In the deserts of life, hearts shrivel up. We can't let others dehydrate from neglect.

Why not clear out a drawer in your kitchen and fill it with stationery, pens, and fun stickers? In between clean-up jobs or while you're watching the potatoes bake, you can jot a little love letter to someone. Get your kids into the act! Teach them early to think of other's needs and reach out in a tangible way. A few words is all it takes. If you know someone going through a long-term sorrow, pre-address and stamp some envelopes so it's easy to jot a thought and drop it in the mailbox once or twice a month.

Be a joy germ and find your own unique way to share a word of encouragement today. Someone you know needs it!

♥

"Dear Lord, we need encouragement, and we need to give it, too. Take our minds and pens and time and use them to uplift someone else, for your glory. Amen."

SISTERSHIP

Patsy Clairmont

Be devoted to one another
in brotherly love. Honor one
another above yourselves.

ROMANS 12:10

Friendship is the ship the Lord often launches to keep my boat afloat. I seem to require people in my life. Scads of them. I am not the type who wants to be an island unto myself. (Unless it's Gilligan's Island.) Not that I don't want to be alone; my alone times are precious to me. I guard them and find solitude necessary for my sanity (well, what's left of it). Yet interacting with others encourages, nurtures, challenges, hones, and helps refine me. My journey has been made more joyous by connecting with friends.

One of my favorite dots in my network of friends is Carol. We are friends with history. We go back to the days when gumdrops were the latest rage in shoes. (Anyone remember those? They were a jazzed-up version of saddle shoes.)

Carol and I still tell each other secrets and giggle over our silly flaws. We know the worst about each other and choose to believe the best. We have not always known how to do that. Then Jesus entered our lives and our friendship. He taught us important skills in esteeming one another. In our thirty-nine years of relationship, we have never not been friends; but since we met the Lord, our friendship has deepened in appreciation and affection.

We love to shop, decorate, antique, travel, dream, and scheme with each other. We have gone through the best of times in our families and the worst of times. We have celebrated and sorrowed together. We have guffawed and groaned. We have worshiped the Lord at the same church and studied the Scriptures in our homes. We have at times let the other one down, which gave us opportunity to learn the imperative friendship skill of forgiveness.

Even though we share many interests, we are opposite personalities. I am boisterous; Carol is reticent. I'm a right-now person; she's an I-can-wait gal. Even physically we are opposites. She towers over my pudgy frame. Her hair is wispy and straight while mine is bushy and frizzy. Differences and similarities along with years of caring and sharing have enhanced our sistership.

Just three weeks ago I moved. I moved only seven blocks, but I still had to pick up everything and find a place to set it down in my new abode — that or have an enormous (thirty-four years' worth of stuff) yard sale. Thankfully, I had dear friends come to my rescue and help me pack.

After arriving in our new home, I was overwhelmed at the prospect of settling in. I had thought I would pull it together rapidly. Instead, I roamed from room to room trying to remember my name. Carol came to give support (and to verify my identity) every morning for four days. She assisted me until early evening, when she would then make our dinner, serve us, and clean up. You can only guess what a gift that was to me emotionally. I never expected that kind of beyond-the-call-of-duty effort, but I'm certain our new home ownership would have found me sinking before I could even unload the cargo, if it were not for Carol's life preserver of kindness.

What is it about moving that is so disassembling? The leaving of the old? The adjusting to the new? The disheveling of all our stuff? The initial sense of unconnectedness? Or all of the above? Carol's and my long-term connectedness served as a stabilizer during this turbulent time. And it was great to have someone with similar tastes to bounce ideas off of about furniture placement, window treatments, and picture arrangements.

By evening, when my wagon was draggin', Carol would catch her second wind and perform wonders in the kitchen. This girl can cook! Every night her feast renewed our strength and our determination to get back at it. The following day we would eat the leftovers for lunch, and in the evening she would prepare yet another culinary delight.

I'm thankful that the Lord knew we would need each other to survive various storms — and that he made available the harbor of friendship.

"Thank you, Lord, that you haven't left me to dog-paddle through life's waterspouts all alone. Amen."

Slippin', Slidin', and Lovin' Every Minute!

Marilyn Meberg

Though he stumble, he will not fall,
for the LORD upholds him with his hand.

PSALM 37:24

"What a fabulous idea! Of course I'd love to ice-skate with you at Rockefeller Center!"

I listened to this enthusiastic declaration from my daughter-in-law, Carla, to my friend Pat the day before Thanksgiving. Pat and I accompanied Jeff and Carla to New York for the holiday weekend, and what a memorable time we had! It truly was one of those experiences this mother-heart has tucked warmly in her cathedral of memories to be revisited many times as the years go by. (Good grief, Marilyn . . . you sound like you're already in a rocker. Get a grip!)

I had no idea Pat had been nursing a desire to ice-skate at Rockefeller Center Thanksgiving morning, and I had no idea Carla even knew how to ice-skate. She happily assured me that she had not skated in twenty-five years but she was sure that would be no problem. "Some things you just don't forget," she explained. Jeff seemed to feel confident about the plan, but I had visions of Thanksgiving dinner at some New York hospital with Pat and Carla in traction while Jeff and I sat alongside eating pressed cold turkey from a metal tray.

But such was not the case! After renting their skates, loading me with cameras and instructions from Carla to "catch a shot" of her skating backwards (something she said she'd never done before but felt might happen "this very day in this very place"), they sailed onto the ice with hundreds of other eager skaters.

I felt enormous exhilaration as I stood rinkside, a part of a scene I'd seen many times on television but never experienced personally. I watched Pat effortlessly glide alongside my lurching daughter-in-law, holding her hand until, within ten minutes, Carla didn't need a hand. I relaxed and started snapping pictures as they waved, bowed, and showed off in various poses meant to depict competence and assurance.

Within a short period of time we at rinkside established a common bond as we shared our experiences about those on the ice. A fifteen-year-old girl stood next to me lamenting the fact that she had not been able to talk her forty-four-year-old mother out of skating today.

"She's never been on ice skates in her life . . . can you believe she's doing this? We come here all the way from Georgia just so she can break her neck in New York!"

I followed the troubled daughter's gaze and found this adventurous mom slipping and sliding along the ice, grinning from ear to ear. Every now and then she was joined by another woman who grabbed her hand, and together they giggled and groped around the rink. "Who's that?" I asked the anxious teenager. "Oh, that's my aunt; she's as crazy as my mom!"

I soon found myself the official photographer for scores of people on the ice, many of whom were skating for the first time and almost all of them from places other than New York. One woman from Alabama who was so exhilarated by her unexpected abilities shouted over to me: "Get a shot of this now!" I got a perfect shot of her posterior just seconds before it hit the ice. She was immediately surrounded by gloved hands that pulled her to her feet. Laughing, she called over to me, "Hope you got that one!"

What an incredible spirit of fun and camaraderie there was at that rink! What was the ingredient that so infused the whole experience with irrepressible joy? Was it the exhilarating, yet biting cold? Was it the uniqueness, beauty, and historical dimension of Rockefeller Center? I think it was all of that . . . but I really believe what surrounded the rink and everyone there was a spirit of caring, kindness, and consistent support. Everyone cheered everyone on. When anyone fell she was immediately helped to her feet and encouraged to continue. We shouted words of praise, clapped in appreciation for every exertion. Even the anxious teenager began to applaud her daredevil mom and "crazy" aunt. There was a tangible sense of kinship — of sisterhood — that seemed to connect us all together.

I think one of the most compelling images in Scripture is found in Psalm 37:23–24. The image of God's extended hand that promises to uphold us provides such sweet security. What better feeling than to be caught before falling by someone who cares about us.

It behooves us all to extend our hand to

each sister who slips and slides her way past us in life. She needs us. And before very much time passes, we'll need her.

"Heavenly Father, you are a God who upholds us, stabilizes us, and never tires of being there. Create within our hearts a broader, more kindly inclination to extend our hand to whomever you send along this slippery path of life. May we lovingly hold each other up and keep each other from falling. Inspire and enable us to 'be there' for each other as you are there for each of us. Amen."

TWENTY-SIX LITTLE SOLDIERS

Luci Swindoll

Do nothing out of selfish ambition
or vain conceit, but in humility
consider others better than yourselves.
Each of you should look not only to
your own interests, but also to
the interests of others.

PHILIPPIANS 2:3–4

All my life, my very favorite human invention has been the alphabet: twenty-six little soldiers ready to do battle at my command. They are all lined up there, neatly in alphabetical order, and when they are called out in squadrons, think of what they can do: they can shout orders, croon lullabies, scream in agony, whisper in ecstasy, dissolve ambiguities, resolve conflict, punctuate pretension, express tenderness, build up, or tear down. They can exaggerate or diminish. They can comfort or control. They can hurt or they can heal.

Twenty-six little letters — the alphabet! Now you tell me a *better* invention. Alone, these individual units are all but meaningless, but when they come together they can change the course of history. And that's often the way we are as people. We need each other. Two are better than one.

For example, let me turn your attention to a wonderful Old Testament passage which explains this very principle. In Ecclesiastes 4:9–12, Solomon expounds on the virtues of teamwork. He says when two work together, they have a better reward for their labor. He makes it very practical, acknowledging that when one falls the other can help him up; when two lie down they keep each other warm. He says that one can be overpowered, but two can defend themselves. This could not be more clear, and I could not agree more.

One of the reasons I like these verses is because the implication is that teamwork is not reserved for challenges of a world-changing nature, but is beneficial in the course of everyday living. For example, the idea of "two are better than one" came home to me a few years ago when a friend and I were traveling together. One day I sat down and actually made a list of why two traveling together was easier than traveling alone:

1. One can pick up coffee while the other watches the stuff.
2. One can navigate while the other drives.
3. One can take care of the other when she is sick.
4. One can do the laundry while the other makes a picnic.
5. One can exchange the money while the other retrieves the baggage.

I see this with my Joyful Journey cohorts. When one of us is tired or not feeling well or burdened about something personal, the others cheer us up. We are there for each other. During the latter part of our conferences last year I had a terrible case of laryngitis, and I can't tell you the times my companions brought me water and cough drops, made me sit down in the only chair available, insisted I rest a bit longer, offered to speak in my place — all sorts of things to make my load lighter. And it was a comfort. The camaraderie and teamwork did as much to lift my spirits as did the water or chair or cough drop. How I appreciate these wonderful, unselfish women.

By reaching out to and supporting one another, we make life a lot more bearable — and more joyful as well. Marilyn, Patsy, Barbara, and I are accustomed to traveling alone when we speak. The Joyful Journey format has afforded us the opportunity to work as a team, which is rather new for us. It has been surprisingly delightful and fun. We didn't even know we needed it, but the camaraderie is unbeatable. I'd venture to say we like that part of our trips the best.

In God's economy you will be hard-pressed to find many examples of successful "Lone Rangers." Remember the power of the individual units of the alphabet coming together, and team up with somebody. Connect with a friend, a companion of your heart. You might be amazed at what you'll discover and enjoy together.

"Lord, thank you for designing me for fellowship — with you, and with others. Help me be a team player so I can accomplish all you have for me to do. Refresh my soul with the love of a friend . . . and refresh her soul with my love as well. Amen."

Rainbow Gardening

Barbara Johnson

An anxious heart weighs a man down,
but a kind word cheers him up.

Proverbs 12:25

When I opened my mail last week, I pulled out a letter with a tiny surprise tucked inside. In a miniature plastic bag was a teaspoon full of colored sprinkles with a label that said: RAINBOW SEEDS. PLANTING INSTRUCTIONS ON BACK. Delighted, I quickly turned over the packet and read:

WHEN TO PLANT: Any season, but rainbows grow best just after a storm.

WHERE TO PLANT: In the light of the Son, preferably near a pot of gold.

HOW TO PLANT: Assume a kneeling position close to the earth. Dig a hole deep enough to hold the cause of your dark clouds. Place the cause and the seeds in the soil, cover with earth, then rise and stomp down with both feet. Walk away in faith.

HARVEST: When needed most.

I got to thinking about how a rainbow is a perfect picture of God's grace. It's a kind of refuge for our mind when storms threaten to rip us apart and flood our dwelling. A rainbow is a multicolored arc formed opposite the sun by the refraction and reflection of the sun's rays in spray or mist. In the rainbow we see God's promise that he will never again devastate life on earth.

But sometimes, in the haze of the clouds after a storm, we don't *see* the rainbow. Well, maybe we need to go looking for it. Maybe the best rainy-day activity is to busy ourselves finding our own rainbow. And when we find it, maybe we can harvest a few seeds and send them to someone else. Rainbow gardening is about growing *encouragement* through reflecting God's light.

Encourage means to puff up or enlarge the heart. As I speak around the country I visualize the hearts in front of me: squashed down, stamped upon, and flattened out from ruthless deeds and lack of care. Into the soil of those hearts I start digging a hole. I use the spade of laughter and throw in a little fertilizer: the story of my own losses. Then I throw in the rainbow seeds and hope each listener will throw in beside them the causes of her own pain. Together we cover the hole with prayer and rise to go our separate ways. Every individual must add her own faith to the mix.

Sometimes I hear about the sprouts that come up. Sometimes I don't. But I've found that people have all kinds of ways to cultivate their own rainbows and spread the joy and hope to their friends and families and communities. Where rainbows grow, angels sing and courage becomes contagious.

Next time you encounter someone in pain, don't just wince and pass by with a shrug. Hurting people need a bit of color to brighten their dark places, and they need to remember the promise that God is with them right where they are. You can be a rainbow gardener by opening your heart even if you're in pain yourself. Let someone know that although you don't have it all together, you find comfort and hope in the Lord.

Take your friend by the hand and wander with her into the mist and clouds of the unknown. Look for that multicolored arc in the sky connecting heaven to earth. Collect your rainbow stories and share them with one another. Let's all create illustrated volumes of our life's best and boldest benedictions, the things we learned in the presence of rainbows.

"Dear Heavenly Father, thank you for the rainbow we read about in your Word. Thank you for the testimony of Noah and his family. You give us a fresh start after every storm. We rest in your faithful love and promises. Amen."

ODD DUCKS IN SILK HATS

Relishing the Peculiar

DID I SEE THAT?

Marilyn Meberg

Keep on loving each other as brothers.
Do not forget to entertain strangers.

HEBREWS 13:1–2

When Luci left her native Texas to move to California nearly twenty-five years ago, there were numerous little culture shocks she experienced as she attempted to absorb the "peculiar" California customs. One of those peculiarities was that our freeways are often littered with chairs, couch cushions, stray clothing, and various other abandoned treasures. Luci maintained that in Texas we would never see junk like that strewn about the freeways.

We would frequently be zipping (that's when I drove) the freeway only to have our conversation interrupted numerous times with Luci-statements like:

"Can you believe that . . . three Tupperware bowls in the middle of the fast lane?" (I don't know how she could know they were Tupperware.)

"How do people lose shoes on the freeway? Does someone simply toss them out? And why only one shoe . . . I don't think I've seen a pair."

"Oh, Mar, look at that little yellow stuffed gorilla. I wonder why it's yellow . . . don't you think it would make more sense if it were brown? I can imagine some little kid feels awful about now. Maybe the mother tossed it out. I don't think I could drive with a yellow gorilla . . ."

One afternoon we were driving back from Los Angeles at a fairly good clip and I noticed a green couch off the edge of the freeway not far ahead of us. Luci and I were involved in a pretty heady conversation which I didn't want to interrupt so without announcement, I switched lanes and pulled off the freeway several feet away from the couch. With unexpressed but mutual understanding, we both got out of the car, walked to the couch, sat down, and continued our conversation.

You should have seen the whiplash responses of people as they hurtled past. They couldn't believe they had just seen two women chatting animatedly on a discarded couch by the side of the freeway.

Later as we pulled back into traffic still laughing, Luci said, "You know, Mar, I wouldn't have missed that for the world!"

"Neither would I, Luci. And just think, if we'd been in Texas, we wouldn't have had a place to sit!"

I am of the firm conviction that one of the most winsome as well as healing ways to love each other is to entertain each other. Now I know very few of you would set up shop by the side of the road while cars whizzed past. But there are so many quiet, perhaps more sane ways of loving through entertaining. For instance, the sharing of little anecdotal experiences while at the cleaners, gas station, your office, driving your car pool, etc. Perhaps you could read to each other some odd, peculiar, whimsical, or offbeat thing you saw in a newspaper or magazine. I know one of the reasons I feel so close to the three ladies with whom I share the platform at Joyful Journey conferences is that they entertain me. They teach and encourage me, too, but oh, how they amuse me! To me, that's loving.

Incidentally, when these joy offerings are handed out to strangers or observed by strangers, we're fulfilling Hebrews 13:2. Now maybe the writer of Hebrews was referring to "at home" entertaining . . . but who's to say we can't take it on the road?

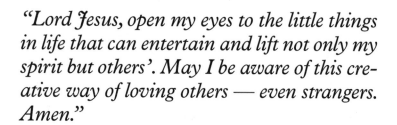

"Lord Jesus, open my eyes to the little things in life that can entertain and lift not only my spirit but others'. May I be aware of this creative way of loving others — even strangers. Amen."

WHERE'S IOWA?

Luci Swindoll

Whether you turn to the right
or to the left, your ears will hear
a voice behind you, saying,
"This is the way; walk in it."

ISAIAH 30:21

Marilyn and I were riding along in her car in the city of Riverside, California. I was navigating with a map of the area as we diligently searched for a short little street named "Iowa." The map wasn't very helpful, actually. Only the major streets were clearly delineated. Finally, after turning the map to the right and left, even upside down, I finally saw in fine print a tiny street called IOWA.

"Turn off on Columbia, Mar," I advised, "then make an immediate right. I'm sure it's down that way." Marilyn did exactly as I said, and after driving for several blocks, still there was no "Iowa."

Marilyn made her characteristic U-turn

in the middle of the street and we started back the other way. While we waited for a red light to change and pondered where on earth this little street could be, a UPS truck pulled up on our left and a beat-up old pickup truck came up on our right. The guy in the pickup yelled through our open windows to the guy in the UPS truck: "Yo, where's Iowa?"

Without the slightest hesitation, the UPS guy yelled back, "Up the street two blocks and to the left. Can't miss it." We could hardly believe it. We looked at each other while we received perfect instructions from two total strangers as they conversed through *our* car. Mar hit the gas, tootled up Columbia two blocks, and found Iowa right where it was supposed to be.

There are times when oh, what we wouldn't give for a little direction. Desperately we long for God's guidance. How many times have I heard people say, "I really want to do what God wants me to do, but what is it? What is his will anyway?" We fret and fume and sit on the sidelines waiting for a skywriter to fly by with the message, "BECOME A MISSIONARY."

I've always believed that those who want to know God's will can know it. It's his responsibility to reveal it. I've never understood nor trusted people who say, "I woke up this morning and my wife was cooking bacon. I *knew* then I was supposed to go to Israel." I think God has more straightforward ways to lead his children:

1. His Word. The Bible is very definitive about the responsibility of a disciple of Christ.
2. Circumstance. God opens some doors and closes others.
3. Wise counsel. Proverbs 13:10 tells us, "Pride only breeds quarrels, but wisdom is found in those who take advice."

And consider this as a rule of thumb: God never calls without enabling us. In other words, if he calls you to do something, *he* makes it possible for you to do it. And, let me go a step further: if you don't sense his strength and ability within you to do it, I would question the call.

If God's Word, your circumstances, and the counsel of others line up, and if you sense his provision, I'd say *go for it*. And don't be surprised if, in some peculiar way, God confirms your call. Somebody in a beat-up old pickup might drive by with just the direction you need.

And if you're looking for Iowa? Give Marilyn or me a call. We know just how to get there.

"I pray, Lord, that I will look for direction for my life only *in you. But because you're the God of the universe, I realize you sometimes show me your way through creative, even peculiar, means. Help me to look and listen carefully to what you might be trying to tell me in some manner I never dreamed possible. May I relish the joy of knowing you are full of wonderful surprises. Amen."*

GOD'S INSTRUMENTS

Patsy Clairmont

Since my youth, O God,
you have taught me, and to this day
I declare your marvelous deeds.

PSALM 71:17

Have you noticed some peculiar quack-ups in Scripture? No, not people, but things that behaved . . . well . . . rather oddly. For instance, Balaam's talking donkey. The only donkey I ever heard chatter was Frances the Talking Mule in the movies, and she (or is it he?) definitely had the benefit of technological intervention.

No doubt Balaam, the rider, was startled when the donkey began to converse, although Balaam continued the conversation without missing a beat. (See Numbers 22:29.) Scripture tells us the Lord opened the donkey's mouth and he (the donkey) said to Balaam, "What have I done to you, that you have struck me these three times?"

(Numbers 22:28). I wonder if our animals have some things on their mind they would like to say to us. If your pet's mouth were opened, what do you think he would proclaim? Perhaps, "What's with the doggie treats? They taste like Styrofoam!" Or, "Call an exterminator; I'm not catching one more mouse in this rat trap." Or maybe, "You haven't cleaned my cage in a week, and you call *me* a bird brain!" The possibilities are endless. I'm sort of glad they are semi-silent . . . for now.

Anyway, back to oddities. I've always thought it strange that the little boy's lunch box (John 6:9–14) turned into a cafeteria for thousands with leftovers. Now there's a lunch that smacks of entrepreneurial possibilities. I bet the Colonel would like to get hold of that recipe.

Or what about the bowl of flour and the jar of oil belonging to the widow who housed Elijah (1 Kings 17:10–16)? No matter how much they used, the containers of flour and oil were not exhausted until the famine was over. It was a gift that kept on giving.

Aaron's budding rod is peculiar to me as well (Numbers 17:8). Here was a branch without soil, sunlight, a root system, or someone to tend it. And what happened? It became an overnight success. It budded, blossomed, and — get this — produced ripe fruit. Now compare that with my lovely poinsettia that I recently received as a gift. When it arrived, it was heady with pink and vibrant green leaves. It was thriving. After forty-eight hours in my home under my attentive care the stems were bald (as in stark naked), and the petals had been humbled to a scraggly, limp, embarrassed, few. So, like Aaron, any tips?

Another quirky situation was when water poured forth from a rock (Exodus 17:6). Rock is nature's strongest, most solid substance. So how did a gushing stream get in there? We aren't talking about a few pails' worth dripping out. Or even a trough full. No, we're talking Niagara Falls. Enough water billowed out to quench the thirst of thousands upon thousands of people and their herds. Whoa, talk about odd.

In that same category of out-of-the-norm events, how about an ark parked on your back forty (Genesis 6:14)? That would surely get the neighbors' goats (and their horses, chickens, and dogs, too). I'll bet that ark was listed in the local newspaper under "Hiraam's Believe It or Not." This wasn't a kayak but a ship-sized vessel that covered a football field. It perched on dry land waiting for an ocean to pass by. Pretty strange.

Perchance when the water floated Noah's

boat it also doused Moses' bush.

Imagine a bush aflame but never consumed by the fire (Exodus 3:2–5). Then add to that God's voice emanating out of it. That would stop me in my tracks, too!

If the talking bush didn't paralyze me with wonder, I'm sure the manna would have (I'm into miraculous meals). What an odd sight it must have been: groceries falling from heaven and dropped on doorsteps. (The closest I came to manna was when I was a kid. We used to catch fresh snow in bowls on our doorstep and add vanilla and milk for our version of heavenly hash.)

The wonder of it all is that the Lord can use everything for whatever purposes he chooses. Not to mention every*one*. I'm amazed he allows a donkey to speak, but I think it's more incredible that he speaks to us at all. For most of the time we are really quite ill-mannered, if not downright stubborn. Yet he chooses oddities and odd ducks for his divine purposes.

"God, help me to see the odd instruments in my life that speak of you. Help me to stay in tune with you so as not to miss any message you send my way. Amen."

GOD'S KIDS

Barbara Johnson

He called a little child and
had him stand among them.
And he said: "I tell you the truth,
unless you change and become
like little children, you will never
enter the kingdom of heaven.
Therefore, whoever humbles himself
like this child is the greatest in
the kingdom of heaven."

MATTHEW 18:2–4

Someone has said that when childhood dies, its corpses are called adults. Research shows that children laugh about four hundred times a day. How many times do you think adults have a good chuckle? Half that many? Or if you're more skeptical, a third as much? Wrong. Adults laugh only about fifteen times a day. That means adults laugh once for every twenty-six times a child has the same pleasure. Somewhere between childhood and

287

maturity, things no longer seem so funny.

Why is that? Could this have anything to do with what Jesus was talking about at Capernaum? What did Jesus mean about humbling oneself to become great? Could it be that as we accumulate the experiences of crisis, disappointment, and stress, the delightful "why's?" of childhood — Why is the sky blue? Why do the birds sing? — become the "why me's?" that rob us of laughter and delight?

Adulthood is full of bad experiences, but there are remedies for the "why me's?" My favorite is to repeatedly expose the person who experienced the bad stuff to the light of as many warm personalities as possible. Another remedy a friend of mine swears by is to hang out with young adults and little kids. In fact, she says, "There should always be a two-year-old in the house." I might not go that far, but I do recommend the light-hearted laughter of children applied consistently to a festering wound.

A darling young mother once gave me the idea to tack up these letters where I will see them — TICDAABGC — and make a list underneath: *THINGS I CANNOT DO ANYTHING ABOUT BUT GOD CAN.* This reminds me there are always things we can't change, but we can get on with our lives and leave those things up to God.

Jesus told us to receive forgiveness for past sins and refuse to worry about tomorrow. In this way, living fully in the present moment, we become more like children with hearts open for laughter and joy.

How do you define childlikeness? A friend wrote, "It's hard to know just when one generation ends and the next one begins. But it's probably sometime around 9:00 P.M." I could relate to that! Maybe increasing my joy quotient will give me the energy I need to get more done *before* 9:00.

Sometimes at the end of a busy day, when I think about all the things I never got around to, I try to look at things differently: upside down, inside out, or with light shining on the dark side. It's like the eclipse of the sun: Most people don't pay much attention to the light — or the lighthearted parts of life — until they are covered by darkness. Then, suddenly, lightheartedness becomes dramatic.

Kids love the way light shines through crystal, ricochets off diamonds, emanates from rainbows. Crystals, diamonds, and rainbows are all designed by God. He put them in the world to remind us to take things *lightly*. He means for us to wonder and imagine what could be hidden in the darkest piece of coal or the rainiest day on earth. As Christians, part of our assignment is to be curious. Kids never think they have all the answers, and we shouldn't either. Thinking we know it all closes our hearts to what is beautiful and new.

Next time you're walking in the dark and feel like you haven't laughed for a long, long time, try standing on your head. Look at your world in a way you've never done before. I guarantee it'll make a kid of you, just the right kind of kid for God's kingdom.

"Dear Lord, keep me from getting so serious about life that I lose my childlike perspective. When things are dark, help me see your light where I least expect it. Amen."

Peanut Butter Yogurt and Raspberry Sauce

Marilyn Meberg

"Go and enjoy choice food and sweet drinks, and send some to those who have nothing prepared."

Nehemiah 8:10

One of the most delightfully peculiar experiences that will be forever squirreled away in my store of memories occurred some years ago when we were living in Fullerton, California.

I was indulging in one of my favorite taste treats: peanut butter yogurt slathered in raspberry topping. As I was just dipping my spoon into this incomparable concoction, the door of the shop opened suddenly and a tiny, elderly lady burst through it. She scanned the shop for a second and then darted over to my table, pulled out the chair across from me, and sat down.

Before I had quite grasped what was happening, she leaned across the table and whispered, "Is anyone following me?" I looked suspiciously behind her and out into the parking lot from which she had emerged. Then I whispered back, "No, there's no one in sight."

"Good," she said, and with that she slipped out her teeth, snapped open her purse, and dropped the teeth into its depths.

Throughout this unexpected scene my spoon had remained frozen between my dish and my mouth. Galvanized into action by the melting of my yogurt, I put the spoon into my mouth. The little lady fixed her eyes upon my spoon and then upon my dish. I asked if she had ever eaten peanut butter yogurt with raspberry sauce. Without ever looking at me, she said that she had wanted to try it all her life but never had. I calculated that "all her life" was probably some eighty years. I asked her if she'd like me to get her some. Without a moment's hesitation, she said, "Yes," but never took her eyes off my yogurt. By the time I returned to our table with her order, she was nearly halfway through my original dish. I found this amusing, especially since she offered no explanation. I started eating what would have been hers, and we slurped along in companionable silence.

Across the street from where we were eating is an establishment for senior citizens that cares for those in fairly good health but in need of watching as well as those in poor health needing constant attention. I classified my little yogurt companion as an inhabitant of this home. The minute she finished her yogurt, she began rapid preparations to leave. She whisked her teeth out from the environs of her purse, popped them in place, and headed for the door.

Concerned about her crossing the busy intersection alone, I asked if she'd let me accompany her. She was out the door and into the parking lot so fast I had to almost run to keep up with her. As I had surmised, she made her way into the senior citizens' building and scurried down the hall. The only thing she said to me was that she had to hurry or she'd miss lunch.

I stopped at the nurses' station and asked the girl behind the counter if she had noticed the little lady I had come with. She said, "Oh yes. That's Felisha . . . she's a real live wire." Then she asked if I happened to be a relative. I told her Felisha and I had just met at the yogurt shop less than an hour ago.

The girl's eyes twinkled as she asked, "Did you by any chance buy her a dish of yogurt?" I was a bit startled as I admitted I had. The girl laughed and told me Felisha knew every trick in the book.

I have revisited this memory many times through the years, not only for the deliciously quirky experience it provided, but for the example Felisha provided. Here's a little woman who knew how to get the most out of life . . . even to the point of my paying for it! I'll confess to you right now that Felisha is my model for "at the Home" kind of living. When that day comes for me, I intend to join as many strangers as I can who will buy me peanut butter yogurt or whatever else they may be eating. According to Nehemiah, that's a scriptural concept!

"Dear Lord Jesus, there's so much in life that isn't fun, that hurts and drags us down. Give us the eyes to focus on the stray joys that could so easily slip past us. Help us widen our vision to not only encompass those joy breaks, but to see the ways in which we can bring them to others in whatever stage of life they may be. Amen."

THAT'S ODD

Patsy Clairmont

O Lord, you have searched me
and you know me . . .
you are familiar with all my ways.

PSALM 139:1, 3

The dictionary describes odd as "strange, unusual, or peculiar; eccentric in conduct; in excess of what is usual, regular, approximated, or expected."

I am fond of this condition called "odd" for it smacks of originality, spontaneity, and sagacity. It takes spunk and smarts not to follow the freeway but to search for what the poet Robert Frost called "the road less traveled."

When I was growing up, I wanted my parents to be "normal." Every time they acted odd I panicked. My goal as a young person was to fit in. Today I look back and celebrate my parents' oddities because they made my folks sparkle with interest and spared me the boredom and blueprint of "normal." (Besides, we all know that normal is just a setting on our dryers.)

When I was a child, I had the painful privilege of living in many homes. Some of them, though lovely, seemed strange and unusual to me. I remember one home in which my bedroom was the recreation room. I would fall asleep at night looking at the padded black and white musical notes strewn across the wall at odd angles.

In the kitchen we had colored appliances that were foreign to my eyes since everyone I knew had white ones. I remember the wallpaper was from France and had French words on it. I always wondered what that mysterious verbiage meant. The kitchen contained a built-in booth, which I thought was cozy but different (none of my friends had booths). The living room had a full wall mural that was soft and attractive, but once again outside of the norm. The carpeting was so thick and deep you could tell who had walked through the room by the size of the footprint left behind. Vacuuming was a full-time requirement to keep the carpeting fluffed and footless. It may have been the impetus for moving, though, for after less than a year we relocated.

The next home was about as normal as

they come (a three-bedroom brick); so my mom soon became bored with it, and we packed up again. That move took us to a fascinating home a couple of miles from where we had been living. Some of the walls in this home were padded and tufted; most were covered in beautiful wood custom crafted by a carpenter for his family. The different woods created the effect of a luxury liner in some of the rooms while others reminded me of a cabin in the woods. My friends thought our home charming but odd.

Today I find odd appealing. It safeguards my chances of settling into a cookie-cutter existence without dynamic distinctives. I enjoy interviewing people and finding out what strange things they have done, places they have lived in, locales they have traveled to, and projects they have worked on. It has been enlightening and even inspiring to hear some of their answers.

One gal, who had also moved a lot, told me her family had the odd history of going repeatedly from rags to riches. Each time they lost everything they would live an opposite lifestyle until they could recoup their finances. During one of their moves back to rags, she and her mom were told they could take only three possessions with them. Her mother selected three paintings. Because of limited space in the vehicle and the long trip in front of them, her dad nailed the paintings to the inside roof of the car. There was no back seat so her dad made her a bed in the back hatch, and on their long journey she traveled staring at the lovely paintings. They lived in their car and ate little sausages out of cans. She confessed she didn't know until adulthood the oddity of their lifestyle. Her somewhat eccentric dad made the arduous trips and shifts in income a grand adventure.

My friend Mary lived in a floating, two-story house in Seattle; a missionary friend lived in a grass hut for awhile; my son's teacher had a swimming pool in the center of her home (all rooms emptied into the pool); and I met a family that lived on an island. There is no end to odd living arrangements or, for that matter, odd homeowners.

Speaking of odd living arrangements, John the Baptist lived in the desert and ate bugs (give me those little sausages any day). His parents were deceased, he wasn't married (I wonder why . . . duh), and he dressed funny. Yet Scripture refers to him as the one who came to make ready the way of the Lord (John 1:23).

Do you feel awkward because something

about you is out of the norm? Maybe it's your looks, your educational status, or your family background. Why not relish your uniqueness? And then trust the One who loves the peculiar to use your life with all its odd variations.

"Jesus, today remind me that no shadows or variations from the 'norm' have reached me that have not first passed through your loving hands. Regardless how odd the circumstances may be, teach me to relish the abnormal and to see ways you want to use it in my life and in others' lives through me. Amen."

GOD'S CREATIVE IDEAS

Luci Swindoll

"Everything is possible
for him who believes."

MARK 9:23

Tax time is usually a drag for most of us. But there are some years when, after April 15, we feel absolutely poverty-stricken. That's how I felt some years ago when my taxes were so high I had little left for the "frivolous" things of life: little luxuries like buying books, taking trips, eating out.

I put myself on a very strict budget for three months, making it a point to write down every cent I spent for even the most insignificant things, like toothpaste or a Coke. I canceled various magazines and newspapers to which I had subscriptions and thought of every way under the sun to cut costs around my house. Actually, if the truth be known, it was kinda fun.

About three weeks into this exacting self-imposed regimen I was praying one afternoon that God would give me a creative idea of how I could have a lot of fun on little money. As I was leaving the home of a friend that evening I noticed she was tossing out a mum plant simply because its blooms were wilting. I felt sorry for the plant and asked her if I could have it. Incredulously, she announced, "But it's dead." I assured her that given enough time, I could revive it. She doubted that . . . which was the only challenge I needed to go full tilt on a new project. *This* was the answer to my prayer. I was going to create a garden, and it wasn't going to cost me a penny.

I was living in a complex where people would often toss their old dead (or dying) house plants in the garbage bins, with no further thought. I began to collect everybody's discarded mum plants. Some had been cut back, but most were just lying there with brown leaves, looking like there was no life left in them. In the course of the next three or four days I must have brought home more than twenty plants in various throes of death rattle, and began nursing them back to health.

First, I cut them all back, watered them, and placed them on the upper deck just outside my bedroom window. I sang to them and played Mozart for them. When necessary, I killed aphids with a concoction of rubbing alcohol, Murphy's Oil Soap, and water. I had become Martha Stewart. My friends accused me of making my own dirt.

I fertilized those precious little plants faithfully. In short, I *loved* them into blooming again. And *did they bloom!* I started taking pictures of them at various stages of growth: with small buds, buds just breaking into blossoms, fully blooming, and finally dying back. At one point, I'll bet I counted seven or eight hundred blooms. Magnificent hues of every color of mum in the world: yellow, orange, white, purple, rust, brown, mauve . . . they were gorgeous! And when people walked by or went outside, they looked up at that array of color. Some pointed, others took pictures, and *everybody* commented about my flower garden.

My friends who had teased me unmercifully about collecting dead plants began asking for *their* plants back. They begged me for mums. "Please, Luci, just enough for the table for my dinner party?" *No way!* Every time I looked at those sweet flowers I was reminded of God's brilliant answer to my prayer.

Have you been down in the mouth lately?

Want to do something fun or uplifting for your spirit, but find yourself with no money to splurge? Ask God for a creative idea. He will give you one, and you will experience a dimension of his giving that is different from the rest. It will be restorative to your soul, because it will once again prove his ability to provide for you, even in odd, zany, off-the-wall ways.

Excuse me . . . I'd like to sit here and chat longer, but it's garbage day so I think I'll go see if I can find a few dead plants.

"Father, thank you that you can create something beautiful out of what appears to be dead. You do it every day. I'm grateful for your creative ideas that cost nothing but demonstrate your love for me. Amen."

MASTERPIECES

Barbara Johnson

"You intended to harm me,
but God intended it for good."

GENESIS 50:20

An English fisherman went into an inn at the end of a long, cold day and ordered a pot of tea. Bragging to friends about his big catch of fish, he stretched out his arm with a sweeping motion. In an instant he knocked the teapot off the table and against the wall. A dark stain splashed across the wallpaper.

The fisherman was aghast at what he had done and apologized profusely to the innkeeper. He tried to wipe off the tea, but already it had made an ugly blotch. Shortly, a man seated at the next table came up and said, "Calm yourself, sir." The stranger took out a coal pencil and began to sketch around the shape of the stain. In moments he created a picture of a majestic stag that looked as if it had been designed for that wall. Soon he was recognized as Sir Edmond Lancier, England's foremost painter of wildlife.

What Sir Edmond Lancier did with an unsightly tea stain in a fine English inn, our God is doing every day. He is working in the lives of people who wonder how they'll ever recover from the ugly things that have happened to them. He is making masterpieces of our lives that stand as testimonies to his love and power.

Just as people began to come from miles around to see the work of Lancier, people will be watching from near and far to see the wondrous things God is doing with the darkest conditions in your life. When I finished writing *Splashes of Joy in the Cesspools of Life* the publisher's sales people wanted me to change the last part of the title to *Potholes* or *Mudholes of Life*. They claimed the Christian audience wouldn't accept the concept of *cesspool* in a book title. I managed to convince them we are talking about *real life* here, and Christians are not immune.

You and I know about the worst and grossest and most detestable things that can possibly happen. But we serve a God who is a Master. He can transform the blackest black to the purest white. He can transform our sin or the results of other people's sins in our lives by his creative artistry. If you don't believe me, start asking around. You won't have to look far to find people who can testify to his redemptive work.

As I hear the stories of thousands of people all over this country, I am amazed at the very different ways God brings good out of what Satan meant for bad. There is no doubt in my mind that if you do not see it in the present moment, it is in process. It's like they say about the weather in England: if you don't like it, wait a minute. There is nothing outside the reach of God. With time and faith, you'll see the majestic head and loving face of Jesus Christ, the Savior, emerge from your life's worst stain.

Now, next time you knock the teapot off the table, remember who is seated in the very next chair. Look for splashes of joy.

"Dear Lord, our Savior, you are the Artist of our blemished lives. Thank you for the masterful way you transform our stains for your honor and glory. Amen."

NO PINK DUCK RIDES

Patsy Clairmont

But ye are a chosen generation,
a royal priesthood, an holy nation,
a peculiar people; that ye should
show forth the praises of him who
hath called you out of darkness
into his marvelous light.

1 PETER 2:9 (kjv)

I once read the quip, "Life ain't no ride on no pink duck." It stuck in my brain like a colorful Post-It note. I have recalled it many times for my own enjoyment as well as a reminder that life ain't easy.

One winter evening, as I walked home from my mother's apartment, a woman from Mom's building was disembarking from her car and expressed her fear of falling on the ice. I asked what I could do to help her feel safe. She suggested I take her left arm while she used her cane in her right hand. We slowly made our way across the frozen patches.

When we reached the curb, she asked, "How old are you?" I told her, and she replied wistfully, "How fortunate you are." Then she stated sadly, "But I must tell you that you don't have a lot to look forward to. Aging is painful." She turned to enter the apartment and pleasantly called out, "Happy Thanksgiving!"

Have you noticed that we are laughter and tears, dirges and dances, jubilations and consternations, hallelujahs and woes? We proclaim, "Life is dreadful" in one breath and "Happy holidays!" in the next. We have good days, great days, and way-down-deep-in-the-pit days. Some seasons are easier than others, while some are downright impossible. I've wondered how some folks have survived the many hardships that have come their way. Others' lives have seemed almost charmed. For each of us, our days are unpredictable, and we tip the scales from preposterous to precious. Life is a gift bulging with mystery, intrigue, comedy, tragedy — and purpose.

When we realize our days here matter, our pain has significance, and our choices are meaningful, we can step through the darkest of times with hope in our hearts. It's not that we won't waver, but even our inquiries have the potential, when we are seeking, to lead us to a stronger faith.

I'm certain the woman in the parking lot was right when she said aging was painful. Yet I also know that the teenage years can be traumatic (mine were). In fact, even my young-adult years were riddled with emotional and relational pain. My sons both told me their most painful school years were during junior high. Does this mean life is a pain? Sure does . . . but thankfully not all the time. Pain is not the only thread in life's tapestry.

Joy must be the shocking pink thread in our tapestry because people seem stunned by this flamboyant stitch. When we exhibit joy during trying times, others view us as odd ducks 'cause everyone knows life ain't no ride on no pink duck.

I find that my joy is enlarged by understanding that, as a child of God, even my pain has purpose. That realization doesn't eliminate my pain, but it makes it more manageable, allowing me other emotions in the midst of calamity, including shocking pink joy.

The Lord has called us to be a peculiar people. Not strange in the sense we act bizarre, but peculiar in the ways we respond to life because the Lord's Spirit is working within us.

Remember Stephen? There was an odd

duck, if ever we should see one. He was chosen from and by the congregation of the disciples to minister (Acts 6:1–6). As a man full of the Spirit, wisdom, grace, and power, he outraged men of lesser character, and they lied to eliminate him and the powerful impact he was having on others. A mob mentality flashed through the group of rage-aholics who stoned Stephen to death. In his last breaths, he called on the Lord to receive his spirit, and then, falling on his knees, this odd man said the most peculiar thing: "Lord, do not hold this sin against them" (Acts 7:60).

It's one thing to eventually forgive unjust behavior, but to ask that others not even be held accountable while one is still in the midst of excruciating, life-taking pain — why, that's downright peculiar. Make that upright peculiar. Stephen was an odd duck (not a pink duck) with a silk hat. His silk hat was the covering of the Lord over his life, which is how and why he was able to be faithful to his last breath. How comforting to read that, after he made his request, "he fell asleep" (7:60).

I know I am a strange and unusual person (many have pointed this out), but I am uncertain how often I am peculiar in an upright sense. This makes me all the more grateful for the One who offers to come alongside and assist me across the icy landscape of life.

"Lord, deliver me from my strangeness and help me to become exceedingly peculiar. Amen."

CHANGES: THE GOOD, THE BAD, AND THE UGLY

Barbara Johnson

Listen, I tell you a mystery: . . .
we will all be changed.

1 CORINTHIANS 15:51

Recently Bill bought me a red lava lamp to put on the TV. When I turn it on it makes the most unusual shapes and patterns as the lava bubbles up into the cone of the lamp. I relax as I watch it slither and shimmy. Its patterns are never the same twice. And just when I think, *Oh, there's an especially nice one,* it changes into something different.

This lamp makes me think of all the patterns and shapes our lives take. Sometimes we bubble up in a nice smooth glob that seems to know where its going. Other times we hit something and break into a jillion little globules that dodge off in a zillion directions. Sometimes symmetrical, bur mostly irregular, our lives are unpredictable, dramatic . . . and always interesting.

Sometimes all the changes drive us crazy. I used to try to get it all together, then gave up. I used to try to keep up, stay on top of things, be always stylish, updated, in touch. Now I know better. I've learned to take circumstances one at a time, a day at a time, and moment by moment bring the constantly swirling mass of my life's lava to Jesus. They say the only thing that doesn't change is the fact that everything's always changing. If that's true (and it is) then we really need Jesus more than ever. He knows how to make change work *for* us.

Psychologists say positive change is as stressful as negative change. Think about that next time your colleague gets a promotion, your sister gets a new house, or your best friend wins the lottery. People to whom good things happen will experience the same kind of bursting, bubbling globules. Their patterns of stress are not better than yours, just different. And if you can't help comparing your life with your neighbor's, just wait until tomorrow. Nobody's life is perfect, and if it is, it won't last.

A thin line separates laughter and pain, comedy and tragedy, humor and hurt. Our lives constantly walk that line. When we slip off on one side or the other, we're taken by surprise. But who said there wouldn't be surprises? Knowing God just means that all the rules will be fair; at the end of our life drama, we'll see that.

Meet every surprise with enthusiasm and the determination to learn from it. After all, there is one thing more painful than learning from mistakes (our own or somebody else's): not learning from them. We never know how things will turn out, but if we know with certainty they will make sense regardless of how they turn out, we're onto something. Much of the Christian life involves playing the role of detective: asking lots of questions of God and each other. What am I supposed to learn from this? How will this motivate me to change? None of us knows all the answers, but the next change might bring us closer.

Sometimes Bill and I sit down together in our living room, turn out the lights, and just watch the red lava slip around. We talk about what we're going to do the next day or the next week. We wonder how to best use our time. We end up looking at each other and remembering what the writer G. K. Chesterton said about why angels can fly: because they take themselves lightly. And we know it's the only way any of us ever will.

"*Oh Great God, you are the changeless one. But sometimes I get confused. Why should my life be so zany? If people really knew, they'd never believe it! Keep reminding me that the ability to transform my circumstances is found in the way I think about them. Keep me contained and buoyant in you. Amen.*"

PRESENT TENSIONS

Savoring Your Moments

LICKETY SPLIT!

Luci Swindoll

"You will surely forget your trouble,
recalling it only as waters gone by.
Life will be brighter than noonday,
and darkness will become like morning.
You will be secure, because there
is hope; you will look about you
and take your rest in safety."

JOB 11:16–18

Have you ever raced so fast through the day
that you find yourself wondering if there really is "the sweet by and by" out there someplace instead of the "toils and snares" of the
moment? Sometimes the concept of rest and
peace seems like nothing more than a luxu-
rious figment of the imagination.

During the thirty years I worked for
Mobil Oil Corporation, hitting the freeway
before dawn and dragging home after dark,
I can tell you there were times I would have
given anything for "the quiet life," whatever

it took. I used to dream of retirement with its golf games, its manicures and pedicures, its ease and victory over the tyranny of racing to and from work. Longing for the good life, I would drive along as various cars cut in front of me, lickety split, threatening my spiritual and mental equilibrium, not to mention the hood ornament that almost became a part of another guy's trunk.

"Lord, get me outta here!" I would scream under my breath in my most sacerdotal tone. (Look up sacerdotal, it's a great word!)

One morning I was in my usual snit-fit to get to work when a young man on a motorcycle raced by on my right and passed through another lane of traffic on his left. Bad move! He was going way too fast to be weaving in and out of cars that way, and everyone was giving him a piece of their mind as he zipped by. My personal loving thoughts were, *That idiot . . . he's not going to make it to the next exit if he keeps that up.*

I drove another hundred yards or so, and then the traffic really began to crawl. *Now what?* As I inched forward I began to see the metal pieces of a broken motorcycle on the shoulder of the freeway. Then I spotted the body of someone covered with a sheet. Same motorcycle. Same boy. Somewhere between where I had been and where I was now, this guy had died.

Needless to say, I was sobered and thought about little else that entire day. Even now, more than a decade later, I can still see that scene in my mind's eye. It gives me pause, partly because of the final tragedy of it all and partly because I know there are people out on that very freeway this minute, racing along just as I was . . . just as he was . . . oblivious to the fact that life is fragile. The freeway is the *last* place we think of slowing down or savoring our present moment. We simply want to get the driving over with, so we tear along with all our gripes and derring-do and madness, sometimes risking our very lives.

Even now, a number of years removed from the life I lived in the fast lane, I sometimes forget that life is fragile. The fact that I have more time to dream my dreams and take my ease is no reason at all to disregard the moment I'm in by preferring to be somewhere else. I have to remind myself that *wherever I am* . . . fast lane or slow lane, in traffic or out of traffic, racing or resting . . . God is there. He is *in* me, abiding in me, thus making it possible for me to be all there, myself.

Every day of our lives we make choices

about how we're going to live that day. Wherever we find ourselves in this fragile existence we need to be reminded that life can be brighter than noonday and darkness like morning because we are living fully in this moment, secure in our hope in the Lord.

Whether you're battling traffic with danger and risk on all sides, or sitting in your rocking chair knitting a sweater for your granddaughter, remember to be *all there*. Wherever you are now is God's provision, not his punishment. Celebrate *this* moment, and try very hard to do it with conscious gratitude.

"Lord, I thank you for this moment . . . this very moment. You have given it to me to fulfill a purpose you've designed just for me. I am alive because you have something for me to do and for that, I thank you. Help me to continually realize that life is fragile. It can be snuffed out lickety split, so don't let me race ahead or lag behind in anything. I want to live fully in the here and now. Amen."

JUST A MINUTE

Patsy Clairmont

"Wake up, O sleeper."

EPHESIANS 5:14

TICK-TOCK, TICK-TOCK. I can still hear the commanding sound of my parents' Big Ben alarm clock. TICK-TOCK. I think our neighbors heard it, too. TICK-TOCK. My dad, a milkman, could sleep through a cattle stampede, and it didn't bother him that the rafters of our house were vibrating in time to his clock's ticker. My mom was hearing impaired, so she just turned off her hearing aid at night. My ears worked fine, thank you, and every tock tended to tick me off.

It's been years since I've had to listen to the drumbeat of a Big Ben, but every once in a while I will look in a mirror, or see old friends (or worse yet, their children), or tell someone how old my children are. Then the TICK-TOCKS start to pound in my brain cells. Time seems either to be in my face or to catapult by me. It can be as elusive as my income or as contrary as my weight. Some minutes drag on for eons while some decades seem more like a fleeting dream. I don't necessarily want to harness time, but I'd like to at least corral it. I know for sure I don't want to snooze through my allotted portion.

I come from a long line of snoozers. We are firm believers in catnaps. I didn't actually hear discussions on this topic when I was growing up, but visual aids I had aplenty. My dad's napping style was definitely the best. He could sleep almost anywhere. His snoring made the Big Ben's ticks and tocks seem more like a purring kitten. Dad had little snorts in the middle of his snores, which entertained us all and sometimes startled him back to reality. Because Dad chilled easily he would form a blanket-tent for himself out of the newspaper just before drifting off. The newspaper, usually the funnies, would rise and fall with each breath, making him an amusing centerpiece in our living room. His naps were never lengthy, but his sleep was deep.

I, too, am a deep sleeper, but I do wake up to an alarm . . . usually alarmed. Some of my relatives, on the other hand, sleep through their wake-up calls. My son Marty could sleep through an air raid — although he's finally come up with a series of rings, buzzes, and blasts that penetrate his sleep pattern and alert him to a new day.

Speaking of multiple alarms, I once slept in a roomful of clocks (imagine the wake-up potential there). I was a guest, and the homeowner was a collector of every size clock you could imagine (minus Big Ben . . . whew!). More than fifty clocks' faces stared down on my bed. Some chimed, one cuckooed, a couple played songs, and all of them ticked and tocked in their own fascinating fashion. A couple of exceptions were part of the lineup. These were windup clocks that hadn't been wound, and for them time stood still.

Have you ever wished you could stop time to extend a precious memory, to savor the moment? I would love to have had extended time to gaze upon my newborn sons; I was so struck with their intricate beauty. If I could, I would have nestled into the moment when our first child uttered, "I love you." I wish I could have freeze-framed the tender look on my daughter-in-law Danya's face when she received her engagement ring from our son Jason. I'd like to journey back and savor the sweet moments spent with Les as we held hands and strolled Lake Superior's shores.

We can't stop time, but we can roll back

the years with our memories. Hmm, I guess, in a way, memories serve as our time card, as a way to recall our days and measure our moments. Memories can tick as loud as a Big Ben clock. They can cause alarm, ring with insight, face us with truth, and even act as a wake-up call. Our yesterdays teach us how to savor our todays and tomorrows.

And we want to savor our moments now — for one day, one glorious day, we will hear the wake-up call of all wake-up calls. Not the TICK-TOCK of a Big Ben, but a big trumpet (trust me, not even snoozers will sleep through this one). Then, folks, time will be no more. We will be ushered into eternity. All time measuring devices (wristwatches, timers, sundials, grandfather clocks, alarms, stopwatches, and even the sun and moon) will be obsolete. Never again will we say, "I don't have time," "Time's running out," "How timely," "Just a minute," or "Maybe tomorrow." We will be unencumbered with time limits, and instead of savoring a memory or a moment, we will savor the Savior . . . forever.

"Help us, O Lord, to squeeze out the best of every tick and tock you have allotted to us. Amen."

COOKIES FOR BREAKFAST

Marilyn Meberg

When times are good, be happy.

ECCLESIASTES 7:14

As we "Joyful Journey" ladies write these devotionals, we are fast approaching December 25. Not only do I feel the need to leave my desk, get out into the malls, and slug my way through the crowds, I am also finding myself full of floating Christmas thoughts and memories. I love those! I am not advocating sitting about engulfed in "Christmas Past" so that "Christmas Present" is not attended to, but I must admit there are many images that beckon my revisiting. One that has been floating around me much of today (I know it was triggered by some melt-in-your-mouth sugar cookies my neighbor brought over this morning) occurred at 4 A.M. on December 22, 1991.

Ken had been diagnosed with cancer ten months prior to this date and wasn't even supposed to be alive. But not only was he alive, he was doing fairly well. He was gaining some of the hundred pounds he had lost and was regaining strength. We entered this particular Christmas with guarded optimism.

A tiny bit of background before I continue: Ken's mom, Edith Meberg, was probably the best cook I ever experienced, and her Christmas cookies literally defied adequate description. To say they were phenomenal is a verbal start but still not superlative enough to do them justice. A highlight of each Christmas was to open the huge UPS box from Seattle which contained her cookie delicacies.

Armed with that information, let's go back now to the morning of December 22, 1991. I am a very light sleeper at best, so I was aware of Ken's restlessness on this particular morning. Aware of mine as well, Ken broke into the silence at 3:50 A.M.: "Marilyn . . . I've got a great plan for us for the next couple of hours."

"Really . . . I assume it doesn't include sleep."

"That's right! The plan for this moment is that I must get up and you are to stay in bed for ten minutes. Then you get up, come down to the living room, and the plan will unfold!"

"Okay, Babe, it shall be as you have said." (My response sounded faintly biblical to my ears . . . I liked it.)

At 4 A.M. I got up and went into the living room where, in typical Ken style, he had a fire going (gas logs . . . no effort), a big pot of tea on the raised hearth, and an arrangement of his mom's cookies on a silver tray with Christmas napkins on the side. He had drawn one of the love seats close to the fire, lit all the Christmas candles, and turned on the tree lights. Christmas music was playing softly in the background.

"Ken Meberg, you have the soul of an artist. What a gorgeous scene!"

With happy enthusiasm, he poured each of us a cup of tea. He then handed me the silver tray of cookies and with a flourish of his hand said, "Eat as many as you like, Madam."

"You mean I can eat cookies instead of breakfast?"

"Indeed you can, my dear. This is a special occasion."

For several hours we sat in front of the fire slurping tea, munching cookies, and giggling like a couple of naughty children. I don't know when I have enjoyed a tea party more, and I don't know when I have had better company. I was intensely aware of needing and wanting to savor those moments with my husband, and indeed I did. In fact, I still do.

"Heavenly Father, you give us many softly beautiful gifts. We thank you for every one of them. Remind us to savor the moments you provide, remembering that each is from you, our Father, given to us in love. Amen."

I LOVE PRESENTS!

Marilyn Meberg

Every good and perfect gift
is from above, coming down from
the Father of the heavenly lights.

JAMES 1:17

"But Luci, people would think I was totally out of touch with reality . . . I mean, there's even the potential of an insanity label with this kind of thinking!"

"Not to worry, Marilyn. Who's going to know? In fact, I'm the only one you've told this to and I can think of only a very few with whom I would feel compelled to share it."

"You're such a comfort, Luci."

I may as well tell you about my insane thinking since you might be one of those "very few" with whom Luci feels compelled to share.

First, a bit of background. As of this writing, November 19, I have begun to enter into that customary pre-Christmas "I find the holidays especially poignant since Ken died" phase. Ken loved Christmas and was exceedingly creative and generous with gift giving, decorations, cooking, and entertaining. He entered into all phases of the holidays with tremendous enthusiasm and exuberance. It is, of course, only natural for me to miss that wonderful energy he infused into the season. But what is embarrassing for me to admit is that I also really miss the fantastic presents he used to give me. Beginning with my nineteenth birthday, Ken had made an enormous production of gift giving. You've got to admit, that's a lot of years to be spoiled by someone.

Well, I don't know about you, but starting about now I receive daily at least four or five catalogs, many of which carry some very beckoning items that activate my Christmas longings. And yesterday, I was sufficiently activated to come up with the plan I feared might label me as dangerously out of touch with reality.

Here was the plan: There were two catalog offerings that not only appealed to my aesthetic side but my practical side as well. In other words, not only did I want them, I felt I needed them. But how could I justify ordering these two items for myself? Wouldn't that be a bit selfish . . . possibly self-serving?

After all, both of my adult children have needs and I delight in doing things for them. Shouldn't I just continue in that more self-less mode?

That is when the questionably brilliant idea struck! Why not order them, wrap them, and put them under the tree with a Christmas tag reading, "To Marilyn from Ken." After all, if Ken were still living he would love to get those items for me. But, I thought, that's going to be a bit unsettling for everyone if, as gifts are handed out, there are two "To Marilyn from Ken" presents! My kids are going to think I've really lost it!

As Luci and I were chatting about this yesterday, she enthusiastically endorsed my idea of "To Marilyn from Ken" and even went so far as to tell me in great detail the various gifts she'd purchased for herself, had gift wrapped, and then, in the cozy quiet of her own home, played her favorite music, brewed a flavored coffee, lit the fire, and had her very own party!

I listened with great interest and then said, "Luci, I love hearing about your private parties for just you from you, but have you ever opened gifts from someone who is no longer living?" She stared at me for a moment and then answered softly: "If it were a present from Ken, I'd open it in a heartbeat!"

Occasionally I must remind myself that all gifts are given to me, God's beloved child, with incomparable love and joy. For me to feel guilty about buying myself something is to forget the original Author of that gift. And if I forget that reality, I may then lose sight of his all-encompassing love for me. Everything good and loving in life has its source in God, including all gifts. Actually, if I were to be theologically sound, I'd write on the Christmas tag, "To Marilyn from God." I love that idea!

"Dear loving and generous Father, what a comfort it is to call you Father and to be your child. What a privilege to be one upon whom you long to shower your many gifts. May I lift my eyes from the earthliness of life and see again the beauty of your gifts for the enrichment of my soul and spirit. May I keep ever before me that greatest gift of all who, more than 2000 years ago, lay in a manger so I might have not only abundant life, but eternal life as well. Amen."

Fresh Starts

Patsy Clairmont

The blood of Jesus His Son
cleanses us from all sin.

1 JOHN 1:7 (nasb)

Saturday night baths were a regular yet big event in my husband's family. The rotund metal tub was pulled into the center of the kitchen where the water brigade would then begin. Nippy tap water was gratefully tempered by the addition of kettles full of hot water off the crackling, wood-burning stove. When the temperature was adjusted, the bath lineup began.

The three oldest boys took their baths first — one at a time. (This was a seniority system.) Then the tub was emptied and refilled for phase two — the three youngest children. My husband, Les, was grateful, in this case, to be the middle child, which made him first for the second round in the Clairmont splashdown. The children who required assistance had a vigorous sudsing from head to toes to give them a squeaky-clean entrance into the new week.

I can only imagine the condition of the water (somewhere between mud and sludge) after child number three finished his bath. These were active children who played, fought, and worked hard in the northern woods of Michigan. How wonderful it must have felt on bath night, after a week of sponging off, to sit and soak in the tub. A savored moment to be sure. Not that they could lollygag, since they all needed a turn, and the temperature of the water was hard to maintain throughout the process. This was not a bobbing-for-apples kind of evening, but a get-down-to-business time. You can imagine, with half a dozen children to be bathed and bedded, the system needed to keep moving. By Sunday morning six well-scrubbed, well-fed, neatly attired children headed for church.

In Les's neck of the woods, they had another way, besides the Saturday night tin-tub special, of dealing with dirt: saunas. Finnish steam baths dotted Les's neighborhood. Little buildings with smokestacks on the outside and stoves full of hot rocks on the inside were the order of the day.

After disrobing in the sauna changing

room (about the size of a telephone booth), you stepped into the inner room and tossed a ladle full of water onto the heated rocks. The rocks hissed in response and shot up puffs of steam that cleansed every minuscule molecule of your being. The faint of heart sat on the low benches while the hearty souls went for the top bleacher. When you left the sauna, you felt as though even your innards could pass a Good Housekeeping white-glove inspection.

I've never taken a bath in a tin tub, but I have taken a number of saunas. I left them feeling soggy, relaxed, and spanking clean. I was a low-bench participant. Cedar boughs were available on the benches to smack yourself to stimulate your blood circulation. I left that for the hearty ones. I'm not into discomfort or stinging swats, especially self-inflicted ones. (I'm more into sweets than swats. I'm your have-another-Snickers gal.)

The issue of cleanliness on this polluted planet is a constant one. Every day we shower, scrub, scrape, soak, and scour in an attempt to stay healthy and socially acceptable. In fact, I have a basket at my tubside filled with cleaning utensils: sponges, brushes, loofahs, pumice, and soaps.

As helpful as these items are, they do not

compare to how clean I feel when I have spent moments in the Lord's presence, especially when I begin with a confession time. When I prayerfully remember my shortcomings, I'm not informing the Lord of anything he doesn't already know. But when I enumerate my failings, I take responsibility before him, and he then releases me from dirty shame, grimy guilt, and scummy sin. I am released from all my present tensions. I am cleansed in the innermost parts of my being where even the sauna's steam can't penetrate.

I can still picture my mom using a washboard to deal with tough stains on my dad's work clothes. Our heavenly Father doesn't have to haul out a washboard when he sees our stubbornly stained hearts. We enter the inner room when we plead the blood of Jesus, and our filthy sins become as white as snow in his presence (and that, my friends, is better than a Good Housekeeping seal of approval).

So willingly hop into his tin tub for a vigorous sudsing. Allow him to bathe you in his purging love. Lollygagging allowed. Sit, soak, and savor the moment — then enter into a new week squeaky clean.

"Dear Lord, you who understand my unclean thoughts, my scuffed attitudes, and my smudged motives, please cleanse me from all my impurity. I confess that I _____ and I _____. Forgive me for the nasty way I spoke to _____. Liberate me from my degrading habit of _____. Thank you for a clean heart and a fresh start . . . in the sparkling name of Jesus. Amen."

A REMEDY FOR THE "IF ONLYS"

Barbara Johnson

My times are in your hands.

PSALM 31:15

Time-management experts report that throughout our lifetimes we spend five years waiting in line, six months waiting at red lights, and one year playing telephone tag with elusive callers. The average American spends six years eating, one year searching for belongings amid clutter, three years in meetings, eight months opening junk mail, and four years doing housework. All this when what we really want to spend time on is living happily ever after!

In our early years we hope and dream of what the future holds. Maybe we focus on the specific direction our gifts will take us and start moving ahead one step at a time. The rest of us meander a bit, backtrack and

340

retrace our steps, take a detour or two, and try to follow the yellow brick road to our destiny. As different periods of our life come to a close many of us find ourselves saying, "If only I had . . ." or "If only *they* had . . ."

The Bible gives us the remedy for all the *"if onlys"* of life. The prophet Isaiah wrote, "Forget the former things; do not dwell on the past" (43:18). He knew God had something in mind: "See, I am doing a new thing! Now it springs up" (43:19).

When you live in the present moment, time stands still. Accept your circumstances and live them. If there is an experience ahead of you, have it! But if worries stand in your way, put them off until tomorrow. Give yourself a day off from worry. You deserve it.

Some people live with a low-grade anxiety tugging at their spirit all day long. They go to sleep with it, wake up with it, carry it around at home, in town, to church, and with friends. Here's a remedy: Take the present moment and find something to laugh at. People who laugh, last.

Another happily-ever-after idea is to celebrate Christmas all year round. Doesn't everyone wish the contagious joy of the holidays would seep into summer? You'll find ways to make it happen if you pay attention to people. See what they're good at and give them a compliment. Pick up on their personal burdens and offer to carry one for a while. Keep smiles ready to hand out. Buy somebody a cup of coffee. Offer a ride, a word of encouragement, a prayer. Drop off a plate of cookies. Donate an hour to a good cause.

And what about those of us who'd like to turn back the clock? Well, we can only wind it up again. Someone said, "Anybody knows the secret of perpetual youth: lie about your age." Somebody else said, "Middle age is that time in life when you bend over to pick something up and wonder what else you can do while you're down there." Sure, we'd like to be younger and stronger again. More resilient. But remember Isaiah? He said to let the past lie. Look ahead. Someone has said, "Don't look back. You're not going that way."

It is never too late to spend time on the important things. It is never too late to do what makes you happy. There is always time to look around and see something beautiful. The secret to using time well is no secret at all. It is summed up in the Alcoholics Anonymous slogan: *One day at a time.* This is not only the best we can do, but the careful design of a Creator who knew what our needs are and how to meet them. Some of us will need to adapt that slogan to: One minute at a time. That's okay. This minute is a gift. As someone said, that's why we call it the present.

"Father in heaven, bless our seconds and our minutes. We consecrate each one to you. Thank you for grace to live and breathe with your promise of redemption for every mistake or mishap. We love you dearly, and in your love we determine to live one day at a time. Amen."

Savoring the Crown

Marilyn Meberg

Children's children are
a crown to the aged.

Proverbs 17:6

Having reached that highly esteemed classification called grandparent, I am not only luxuriating in little Ian's current development, but I'm looking back nostalgically to that of Jeff and Beth's some twenty-five years ago.

It was tremendously important to both Ken and me that I not work outside the home until both children were at least in school. I am thrilled that Beth and Steve are of the same mind. The crucial issues of security and trust are established in the first few years of life, so experiencing less than a warm and trustworthy environment in those beginning stages of living can be devastating to the development of a little psyche.

Nevertheless, there were many times when I felt utterly trapped in my mother-

and-child environment. Three days a week Ken would go directly from work to USC for classes. I had no car, was not even within walking distance of a grocery store, and frequently wondered if there was anyone in the world without a pacifier in his mouth. Though I would not have had my life any other way (except to have a car) I occasionally allowed the ever-presentness of parenting to interfere with the savoring of those priceless "kid-comments" that only later did I recognize as precious. Let me give you an example.

I don't know if Jeff was three or four when this happened (I do know he had given up his pacifier because I could see his entire face). I was attempting to instruct him in how to tie his shoes, which is no small task to explain and no small task to understand. Jeff's spirits were faltering, and I was beginning to tire of my own voice. In fact, I was tiring of not having the opportunity to verbalize anything more lofty than how to tie a shoe.

Yielding to a desire for more high-flown language and tone, I startled Jeff by suddenly launching into a diatribe about England's darkest hour during World War II when the people were close to losing heart, fearing they would soon be defeated by the seemingly invincible forces of the German army. "But," I declared, my tone rising, "there was a lone voice in the midst of all that perilous uncertainty: the voice of one of the greatest statesmen in world history. His name was Winston Churchill. It was he who inspired his people over and over again with the words: 'Never give up — never . . . never . . . never . . . never!' "

Noticing Jeff's incredulous little face for the first time since I had gone off into my dramatic rendering, I simply concluded by saying: "So, Jeff, you must never give up — never . . . never . . . never . . . never!"

All that expenditure of energy required a cup of tea, so I retreated into the kitchen, refamiliarizing myself with my life. Upon my return to Jeff's bedroom, teacup in hand, I saw him hunched over his little black tennis shoes muttering resolutely, "Never give up — never . . . never . . . never . . . never!"

As I look back on my years of mothering, my biggest regret is that all too often I did not savor the moments. I was far too concerned with efficiency, tidiness, and order. Now, if I had it to do again, I'd spend as much time as Jeff wanted at the tropical fish store; so what if dinner was late! I'd listen more closely to Beth's endless fiction about a Gertrude Sweatstein and Dr. Bloodworth, whose soap-opera lives she made up were undoubtedly reflections of some of Beth's own eleven- and twelve-year-old tensions.

I guess one of God's ways of giving second chances is allowing us to become grandparents. Because you can bet your last gold filling that if little Ian wants my lap, my ear, or my last ounce of energy or creativity, he's going to get it. I wish I had been that consistently generous with his mama.

"Oh God of patience, kindness, gentleness, and graciousness, enable us to be quiet long enough to hear the faltering steps of the little people who attempt to follow us. May they see in us your patience; may they experience from us your kindness; and may our voices reflect your gentle graciousness. Thank you for the privilege of participating in the molding of their characters. May we rise to that highest of callings and savor each blessed moment. Amen."

WHAT TIME IS IT?

Patsy Clairmont

There is an appointed time for everything. And there is a time for every event under heaven.

ECCLESIASTES 3:1 (nasb)

Sometimes I feel as though there just isn't enough time for all I want to do. In recent years my interests have diversified (or should I say scattered?). But I realize the sands in my hourglass are sifting at such a pace that I can't possibly chase every whim. I don't have time to become a master gardener, gourmet cook, interior designer, carpenter, pianist, and scholar-extraordinaire. Besides, who would like me if I could do all that?

To do too much is as dangerous as to do nothing at all. Both modes prevent us from savoring our moments. One causes me to rush right past the best of life without recognizing or basking in it, and the other finds me sitting quietly as life rushes past me.

No, I'm not so foolish that I'm going to chase pipe dreams — but rainbows, now that's another story. I know I want to be more than I am today. That means I'll have to use my time wisely, invest myself discerningly, and savor the flavor of every delicious moment assigned to me.

Scripture tells us that there's a right time for everything. Then Solomon lists the times. Let's check in with Sol's "clock" (hear it ticking?) and decide what time it is for us:

a time to give birth (I don't think so.)
a time to die (Hmm, closer.)
a time to plant
a time to uproot (Does this mean I have to move again?)
a time to kill (Huh?)
a time to heal
a time to tear down
a time to build up
a time to weep
a time to laugh (All right!)
a time to mourn
a time to dance (The macarena? Nah.)
a time to throw stones
a time to gather stones (Like diamonds, emeralds, rubies?)
a time to embrace

a time to shun embracing (Hello, teens, are you listening?)

a time to search

a time to give up as lost

a time to keep

a time to throw away (Hey, have you been looking in my closet?)

a time to tear apart

a time to sew together (Uh-oh, I don't do thread.)

a time to be silent (Me?)

a time to speak (Now you're talking.)

a time to love (Smile.)

a time to hate (Shudder.)

a time for war (Sob.)

and a time for peace (Whew.)

That's a lot of savoring. Did you find yourself on Sol's list? What time is it in your life? Perhaps you have a giant problem and it's your time, like the shepherd David, to throw stones. Or maybe you've been mourning the loss of a loved one, a broken dream, or finances, and it's time to step into your dancing slippers. You may be in the midst of a relational fracas, and you know in your heart enough is enough: it's time to mend what has been torn apart. Is there someone you've been shunning with your displeasure? Then for you, it's time to embrace.

Whatever your time, whatever your season, even in the midst of tragedy, there are moments worth savoring. Some of us have more sand on the bottom of our hourglass than on the top. (I'm not referring to our figures, even though they do tend to slip with the sand.) Yet, as long as breath is in our bodies, there will be moments, sweet moments, to revel in. This time is our time. Let's go savor the flavor!

"Lord, teach us to enter into the gift of life. Amen."

Enjoy the Ride!

Barbara Johnson

For a thousand years in thy sight
are but as yesterday when it is past,
and as a watch in the night.

PSALM 90:4 (kjv)

Yesterday is a sacred room in your heart where you keep your memories. Here you cherish laughter from another day. You hear melodies of half-forgotten songs. You feel the warmth of a hug from an old friend. You see the lingering glow of a long-gone love. From your yesterdays you draw lessons and encouragement to pass along to others.

My heart smiled at some yesterdays recently when I thought back on teaching my oldest son, Tim, how to drive. We practiced in a nearby cemetery where it was quiet, the posted speed limits were very slow, and traffic was sparse. *A nice, safe place to start,* I thought.

Tim would work his way around the curves and turns, carefully maneuvering the car through its paces. Brake into the curve. Gently. Accelerate out of the curve. Slowly. Smoothly. Stop. Reverse. Back up. Park between the lines. Try it again. Start all over again.

Afterward, we'd go over to In-N-Out Hamburgers across the street where I would recover from the experience. After we ate, Tim would want to tackle the curves again. Sometimes I wondered if I would survive until he actually learned to drive.

Well, I did. Tim did learn. And he was a good driver. But years later, his car was smashed by someone who wasn't. Now, Tim's grave is right up there where he practiced driving.

I could be bitter about it. Or I can be better. When yesterdays bring bittersweet memories, I can fume and blame my losses on someone else, or I can let my memories comfort me and provide encouragement to someone else.

As I was standing by Tim's grave recently and thinking of the many times we wound around those curving lanes, I remembered how I used to feel: nervous and tense but trying not to show it. My reverie by Tim's headstone was interrupted when a little red Nissan came around the curve. There was a mother, about thirty-five, her hair blowing in the breeze. Beside her, in the driver's seat, sat a boy, about fifteen, cute as anything. The mom's face looked intent while the boy tried to look nonchalant.

I wanted to shout out, "Enjoy the ride! Now! Make a memory of your experience. Go get a hamburger to celebrate. Do it now, while you still can look each other in the eyes!"

Yes, it hurts. I wish Tim were here, driving me to some of the places I need to go occasionally, just for old times' sake. I long for the family circle — unbroken — the way it will be in heaven. I want to hear my boy's laughter again and the way he used to rush in the house and call, "Mom!" I envy that mom in the little red Nissan, but I know the years end up stealing something from everybody. And I just want to tell that woman to savor the moment. Taste the present full strength. Do everything you can to hold it close.

This week when I go do the things I have to do, I'll take my own advice. I'll look people in the eyes, and if they don't have a smile, I'll give them one of mine. I'll make a date with my husband or play a joke on a friend. I won't let time pass without re-minding myself, "Enjoy the ride!"

"Dear God, I'm ready for adventure. Let's make a memory! Amen."

GIGGLE BREAKS

Practicing a Laugh Lifestyle

THE SECRET OF FUN

Luci Swindoll

We proclaim to you what we
have seen and heard, so that you
also may have fellowship with us.
And our fellowship is with the
Father and with his Son, Jesus Christ.
We write this to make our joy complete.

1 JOHN 1:3–4

I have friends in Orlando, Florida, with whom I spend several weeks a year, including some holidays. When I visit them, we often go to one of the theme parks in the area. I can't tell you the times I have seen various families in those parks and observed this pattern: The children get tired and their whining turns to crying. This frustrates the mother, who fusses at the children. This irritates the father, who yells at the mother. I can just imagine what he's thinking: *I paid all this money and took all this time off and nobody appreciates it. When I get this bunch home, I'm never taking them anywhere again.*

As I sit on a park bench, peacefully sipping my lemonade, my heart goes out to them. Quite honestly I think everybody would be happier if they *had* stayed home.

Then I reflect on my childhood and our family vacations. We used to go to my grandfather's little bay cottage for the week or two my father had off from work. It was a modest cabin with few amenities and small rooms. Together, however, we had a wonderful time. In the mornings we fished, catching enough for a fish-fry lunch. In the afternoon we took naps, played checkers, and read; and in the evenings after dinner we told stories and jokes, put on little plays, and sang to the tune of Daddy's harmonica. In very simple ways we entertained ourselves and each other.

Since my older brother was interested in science and magic, he performed tricks and displayed his scientific wizardry while holding us in rapt attention. (He loved a captive audience.) When there was no moon, sometimes we kids were permitted to go floundering with Daddy. Boy, that was fun! He carried the Coleman lantern, swinging it back and forth as we waded about mid-calf along the shoreline. When a flounder was spotted, one of us got to gig him.

I remember a couple of times when the boys went and Mother and I stayed back at the cabin. We watched from the bedroom window, singing duets as that swinging lantern disappeared out of sight. What a memory. Even now, as I write this, I can feel a full smile on my face.

Those vacations were not perfect, of course. As three very fair-skinned children, we spent half the summer burned to a crisp and the other half peeling. I'm sure there were tears and fussing and probably some irritation, but the experience of those days is incomparable in my memory.

I've often thought it is impossible to quantify a memory by the amount of planning or money spent to make it. Wonderful memories are made when the spirit is right. Therefore, it doesn't take a lot of money or an exotic setting. What it takes is an atmosphere where people can simply connect with one another. Those connections are powerful, regardless of the circumstances.

The next time you think about getting away with your loved ones, make sure you have built in times to be together. Set aside time to sing, tell stories, entertain each other . . . and laugh a lot. Create memories for yourself and your loved ones. Figure out nutty things to do that will entertain the whole family. Practice a laugh life-style. You can have fun anywhere. Sometimes, I even enjoy myself at a theme park in Orlando.

"Oh Lord, as I think about joy and fun, I am reminded of 1 Timothy 6:17 that instructs us not to trust in the uncertainty of wealth but to put our hope in God, who richly provides us with everything for our enjoyment. Thank you for the laughter you create in the fellowship of being together with those we love. It is a gift of your grace. Amen."

A DIVINE PRESCRIPTION

Marilyn Meberg

A cheerful heart is good medicine,
but a crushed spirit dries up the bones.

PROVERBS 17:22

A number of months ago I received a letter from a group of women who had attended the Joyful Journey conference in Atlanta. These dear ladies are in their mid-seventies, widowed, and "kind of take care of each other." Apparently they gather together each week for a Bible study and then go out to lunch. (Sounds like a fabulous double feed to me!)

They loved the Joyful Journey conference and wanted me to know specifically how they had utilized something I had taught. To one of their scheduled times of sharing and study, two of the women came feeling unusually intense arthritic pain, one had a headache that had been hanging on for days, one felt mildly depressed, and the other two said they felt basically indifferent about everything in life . . . even lunch. (Red flag right there!)

Realizing this was not going to be an upbeat day for anyone, the unofficial leader of the group and writer of the letter to me suggested to her friends, "Why don't we do that fake laugh Marilyn showed us — you know, the one that put everyone in the auditorium into hysterics?" (In one of my talks I demonstrate how the smallest giggle, when practiced on purpose, can lead to belly laughter within minutes.) Out of desperation, these six decided it certainly couldn't hurt anything so they started the fake "heh-heh." It sounded so dumb in their ears that they did end up in genuine fits of hearty laughter.

To their amazement, the arthritic pain lessened, the headache became less intense, and the depression and indifference seemed to give way to a feeling of greater well-being. The writer told me that now they begin each of their weekly sessions with prayer, self-induced laughter, and then Bible study. Needless to say, I was touched and pleased by this testimony of God's healing touch from laughter.

When God said a joyful heart (or laughing heart) is good medicine, I believe he was literal in his meaning. The medical world has verified that laughter releases endorphins, God's natural painkillers, which are fifty to one hundred times more powerful than morphine. So when these dear women all experienced a lessening of both physical and emotional discomfort, they were simply taking their God-prescribed medicine.

You are probably aware that the scientific world has been doing a lot of research about the mind-body connection, especially in the realm of laughter. I was fascinated to read an article in the August 11, 1996, London *Times* (Luci sent it to me — I never go anywhere). A researcher named Jonathan Leake has been seeking the answer to why people who laugh live longer. He has discovered how a group of life-enhancing chemicals are triggered by peals of laughter. These hormones are so powerful, they can energize a person's entire immune system and help it ward off diseases, including the common cold or flu.

In the same article it was reported that Arthur Stone, a professor of psychoneural immunology at the State University of New York who has pioneered research on the effects of laughter, has published a paper outlining the most conclusive evidence yet of a link between laughter and blood levels of immunoglobulin A. (This helps people fight illness by marking invading bacteria and viruses for destruction by white blood cells.)

The search for such organic substances began a decade ago with the discovery of a link between a cheerful outlook and longevity. It was quickly established that melancholy people had higher levels of hormones known as cortisones which are associated with stress and can damage people's ability to fight disease. Only now is the role of their uplifting counterparts, the cytokines, beginning to be understood.

Don't you love that? The God of the universe has said all along that a joyful heart is good medicine. God has given us a prescription for joy. All we have to do is fill the prescription.

"Oh God in heaven, you love us so completely that you even provide a means by which we can be released from pain and discouragement through laughter. How mind-bogglingly creative! Help us to rise up out of the dark corners of our soul and believe you have indeed provided medicine for joyful healing. May we take at least one dose every day. Amen."

SNICKERING

Patsy Clairmont

A joyful heart makes a cheerful face.

PROVERBS 15:13 (nasb)

I was speaking in Colorado Springs in late October, so Les was left at home to give out Halloween treats to any tots who might toddle to our door masquerading as bunny rabbits. That evening he received a dinner invitation too good to pass up, which meant he didn't hand out the bags of goodies he had purchased earlier that day.

I realized we would both look like bloated goats if I didn't get rid of the mountainous candy stash. So one day, as I headed out the door, I filled my pockets with Snickers bars. I had to do some errands in town, and everywhere I went I handed out these miniature candy bars. To friends, to strangers, to salespeople, to women, to children, to men. Without exception they not only were surprised by an unexpected treat, but they all also snickered. Something about the gift caused them to pause, smile, and release a little giggle.

Now, my giving away the candy bars was not what you would call a sacrificial act. But what started initially as a way around my own undisciplined appetite ended up as a reminder for me of how little it takes to brighten a day and a countenance. It was almost as if I had given some people permission for one moment to take a break from the rigors of life and lighten up.

My Mamaw (grandmother) loved peppermint candy. Her somewhat intense personality would brighten if you offered her one. She was not a big eater. In fact, Mamaw would make one plate of food last several days. She was a selective (picky) eater, and not surprisingly she had a lean body frame (some might say bony). But hand her a peppermint, and a smile as wide as her home state of Kentucky would flash across her grateful face.

What does it take to make you unplug from your intensity and giggle? A child's antics? A pet's predicament? A malapropism (now there's a word to bring a smile)? An unexpected note? A rainbow? A bumper sticker?

Barbara is Queen of Bumper Stickers. She

has a collection of fun-filled sayings that folks from all over the country have sent to her, and when she shares them in her talks, audiences just hoot. They get the biggest kick out of these quips that succinctly capture some aspect of our lives in unexpected ways. The bumper stickers kind of zing us, and for a giggly moment we get a reprieve from life's crowded highways.

On those highways I have had the privilege of meeting some exceptional people — generous people who give not only store-bought gifts, but also the gift of themselves. For instance, my friend Ginny Lukei is an ingenious gift giver. She loves to surprise people with presents and activities specifically designed with that person in mind. Her gifts are not hastily thrown together to get an obligation over with (I've been guilty of that) but are carefully crafted to bring joy to the recipient.

One gift Ginny has given me many times is her potato rolls. These will make one giggle with delight and jiggle with extra tonnage. You have not fully lived until you have eaten some of these plump, melt-in-your-mouth-and-head-for-your-thighs rolls. Just to think of them causes me to salivate. One time, because it had been so long since we'd seen each other (she lives in California and I live in Michigan), she made a batch of potato rolls and shipped them to me. Only problem was I wasn't home when they arrived, and by the time I returned days later, the rolls were wearing moss-green fur coats. I didn't salivate — more like regurgitate. Green did not become them (or me). More recently I flew to Ginny's and once again indulged myself in her freshly baked potato rolls . . . and I have the thighs to prove it.

Sometimes I delay offering a gift until I can afford just the right thing, when often the right thing is as affordable as a phone call, a card, a song, a poem, a potato roll, or a Snickers. In fact, I think we should declare today Snickers Day from this moment hence. C'mon, girls, load up your purses, briefcases, and tote bags with candy bars for others and let's go on a Snickers toot. Betcha a potato roll that faces will light up, and instead of sighs, for one brief moment you'll hear the joyful sound of giggles.

"Lord, I'm so grateful you designed us with the capability to giggle. What a pleasing sound. And what a delightful feeling. Help us to be generous with our giggles and sparse with our frowns. In the pleasing name of Jesus, Amen."

TICKLE ME, PLEASE!

Barbara Johnson

"The joy of the LORD is your strength."

NEHEMIAH 8:10

He's a giggling charmer. At Christmas last year, Tyco manufacturers in China worked round the clock and still couldn't keep Elmo, the tickle-me toy, in stock. At eighteen inches tall, the doll that laughs when you squeeze his tummy costs a whopping $27.99. But shoppers couldn't seem to get enough of the furry little red guy.

"We could sell 100 a day," said a Toys 'R' Us employee in California. In 1996 Elmo's makers shipped one million — four hundred thousand more than expected — around the world. "Nobody can predict a phenomenon," said the company's president.

It seems we're all hard up for a laugh. Laughter sells. Giggles sell. Tickles and tee-hees are what we all want. Tune into the toy market. Turn on the TV. As our world grows darker and more despondent, more violent, more at odds with our ideals, we turn to manufactured laughter to cope. It gets us through tedious days, lonely evenings, and now, it seems, even playtimes. We depend on fuzzy red dolls because we've forgotten how to laugh from our hearts.

In the old days, people said that the only fun we have is what we make ourselves. And old-timers got creative to make it happen. Today we have store-bought games, hours of sitcoms filled with suggestive jokes followed by canned guffaws, and, for the little ones who haven't learned from us about real belly-busting laughter, we have Tickle-Me Elmo dolls.

What happened to rubbing shoulders and slapping knees and creating an evening of warm hilarity based on our fellowship with each other? Have we forgotten how to be silly? The Bible says a merry heart is good medicine (Proverbs 17:22). Judging from experience, I think we all need an extra large dose.

What makes you laugh? We all have a slightly different sense of humor; different things are funny to different people. Get to know yourself. Drag out the books and jokes that make you chuckle. Find friends who spare no mercy as they get you to giggle uproariously. Tune into people wherever you meet them who make you smile.

Then turn it around. Laughter is contagious. Seek out ways to make your friends and family smile. Everyone is just like Elmo: we're all crying, "Tickle me, tickle me, please!" We're all desperate for the good medicine of laughter. There's not one of us who can't use some extra joy.

When's the last time you made someone laugh right out loud? That ability is built into every one of us, just in different ways. First of all, we have to relax. I love that line from the movie *The Way We Were* where Robert Redford tells Barbra Streisand: "Everything that happens doesn't happen just to you personally."

Remind yourself to loosen up. Try not to take everything so personally or so seriously. Shake off offenses. Let go of what you perceive as an insult or insinuation. Lighten up. Chill. Don't have a cow. (Isn't that what the teenagers say nowadays?)

Once you loosen up, let yourself be who you are: the wonderful, witty woman whom God will use to encourage and uplift other people. You're entering a new dimension of joy that will enable you to rise above your circumstances and bring someone else with you. Catch yourself being funny. Give yourself a pat on the back every time someone smiles back at you. Challenge yourself to make even the most sour person grunt out a small chuckle or at least turn up the corners of her mouth.

It's a great day to laugh. Go for it. Tickle me, please!

"Dear Lord, you gave us a funny bone so we would use it. You gave us belly and facial muscles with which to laugh. I won't let them atrophy. I'll laugh with you and for you today. Amen."

BE YOUR OWN SOURCE OF COMEDY

Luci Swindoll

We rejoice in the
hope of the glory of God.

ROMANS 5:2

Five years ago I put a sum of money in Fidelity Federal Bank and locked it into a certificate of deposit. This October it came to maturity, and I had to make a decision whether to lock it in again or take the money out. With my financial advisor's advice I determined that it was time to take it out, and I set the wheels in motion to do that through the mail.

In conjunction with this CD I had also opened a little checking account in Fidelity Federal in the amount of $500, with the assurance that if that minimum amount was kept in the account at all times, I would receive a quarter of a percent interest which would also go into the CD account. Not a big sum, but worth having the account, nevertheless.

Well, once I determined to reinvest the CD proceeds elsewhere, this freed me, I reasoned, to take out the $500 as well. I was thrilled. Here I would have $500 that I'd sort of forgotten about (since I couldn't touch it anyway) to play with. "Christmas is coming," I thought. "This is great timing!"

About three days before the CD transaction was to be made I received in the mail a statement from my checking account, advising that an interest charge of $11.88 had been levied against that account, which not only brought the sum below the $500 I had carefully left untouched, but had come to me out of the blue. I simply couldn't understand why on earth I would get such a statement. *Why, I haven't even used this account,* I muttered to myself. *I've never even written a check. What does this mean anyway? I hate this.*

Well, I thought, *I'll just go to Fidelity Federal and set things straight.*

The next day on my way to speak at a university, I passed a branch office of the bank. *I'll stop there on the way home and clear this up,* I said to myself as I drove by. Which is exactly what I did. I parked in front of the bank, grabbed the statement, flounced inside, marched right up to the teller, and pontificated, "You know, I don't understand this. Here I get this statement in the mail informing me of a charge of $11.88, but I've never even used this account. I mean, this is crazy. I'd like you to waive this service charge, please, and give me a check for $500 right now. Will you do that?"

The whole time the woman behind the counter had said nothing, just looked at the paper, then at me. When I finished blasting out my request she finally said, "Well, I'd like to, lady, but this is Wells Fargo Bank."

The village idiot, crawling out the bank's side door, heard the tellers whispering among themselves: "Can you believe that woman came in here demanding money, and she doesn't even have an account in this bank? Can ya beat that?"

I got in my car and laughed my head off. What else could I do but enjoy my own mistake?

We've *got* to be able to laugh at our own mistakes. At least I do — I'm so experienced at making them.

Don't take yourself too seriously. It just makes life all the harder. It'll all come out in the wash anyway, because God's glory eventually will eclipse everything that goes wrong on this earth.

Lighten up and learn to laugh at yourself. None of us is infallible. We make mistakes in life, and more often than not, they're funny. Sometimes, being your own source of comedy is the most fun of all.

"Jesus, help me to see the humor in everyday occurrences. And when I make mistakes, remind me it isn't the end of the world. It's a learning experience, an opportunity to laugh and to trust your sovereignty. Amen."

A FIRM FOUNDATION

Marilyn Meberg

He brought out his people
with rejoicing, his chosen ones
with shouts of joy.

PSALM 105:43

Ken Meberg was one of the funniest men I've ever known. In fact, what drew us to each other at the tender ages of nineteen and twenty at Seattle Pacific College was our mutual appreciation of each other's humor.

As our dating relationship grew and became more public, Ken and I were walking across campus one day as Dr. Swanstrom was walking toward us. He was not only one of our favorite professors, but probably near the top of every student's preferred list.

He stopped in front of us and with a warm smile observed, "Well, this looks to be getting serious. Is it?" I smiled demurely as Ken agreed that it certainly was in his mind. With twinkling eyes and a friendly clap on

Ken's shoulder, Dr. Swanstrom said, "I just can't imagine the kind of children you two will produce!" Somehow, we felt complimented.

Years later, having produced two children, Ken, Jeff, Beth and I were about a half block from home one afternoon when Ken simply pulled the car over to the curb, wordlessly opened his door, got out, and began walking in the direction of our home. Within seconds I, too, got out of the car and began walking. Jeff, taking his cue, got out of the backseat and headed for home. This left our puzzled seven-year-old, Beth, alone in the car. As she watched us walking toward home she finally called out from the back window, "Don't you think I'm too young to drive?"

One evening as we were eating dinner together, Ken, having scooped out his baked potato from its jacket, simply tossed it over his shoulder where it landed in the far corner of the kitchen. Within minutes, Jeff tossed his empty potato skin over his shoulder. Beth, who was somewhere in the vicinity of five years old, looked at me with undisguised pleasure and said, "They're being childish, huh, Mama?"

"They certainly are, Beth."

With a happy smile, she tossed her potato

skin over her shoulder and proclaimed, "I'm supposed to be childish!"

These and many more times are wonderful memories I hold in my head as evidence of a somewhat zany but fun lifestyle we practiced in our home.

Because I have so frequently used the themes of joy and humor in my writing and speaking, I'm often asked to give pointers on how to develop a laugh lifestyle. I always find that a difficult question because a laugh lifestyle is so much more than tossing potato skins around the kitchen. It is also so much more than joke books, funny tapes, or humorous movies. They have their place and can certainly provide wonderful times of laughter, but the humor they inspire is external to who we are.

The development of a laugh attitude begins internally. It begins with a foundation that is God-inspired and God-constructed. That foundation gives us security as we stand confidently on the strength of his incomparable love for us. Faith in that solid foundation then leads to personal rest and divine security. Without this internal peace, the laughter inspired by all the zany antics we can think of will ultimately die in the wind, leaving a hollow void waiting to be filled with the next antic or joke.

I guess if I were to reduce all of these words about developing a laugh lifestyle into one sure first step, it would be: Become personally acquainted with the Author and Giver of joy. His name is Jesus.

"Lord Jesus, without you our laughter would quickly become hollow and meaninglessness. But you give us reason for being, you give us significance in being, and you fill our being with the awesome assurance that we have been cleansed and forgiven of all sin. Because of the cross, we have been reconciled to you for now and all eternity. Because of that truth we do indeed break forth with rejoicing and shouts of joy. Amen."

THE GOD WHO SEES

Barbara Johnson

She gave this name
to the LORD who spoke to her:
"You are the God who sees me."

GENESIS 16:13

Hagar, the pregnant maidservant of Sarah, had fled into the wilderness. She just wanted to die. But God sent an angel who found her and told her to go back home even though it was the hardest place to go. He then predicted that the child born to her would be a wild man who wouldn't get along with anybody.

Now I don't know about you, but if I were Hagar, that's not exactly what I would have wanted to hear. Hagar's response, however, was to call God a name that had never been used before: *The-God-Who-Sees*. And she accepted what he said.

Yes, our God is the all-knowing One who sees our scars, our secrets, and our strength.

Our wounds and shame are his affair, and he knows just how much trouble we can stand. Somehow, the fact that he knows us so well makes a difference. We understand there is a direction and we are part of a bigger picture. From the wildernesses in our lives, the fact that *he sees* gives us a reason to carry on. No longer are we anonymous, lonely, and lost.

I wonder what kind of reception Hagar got when she returned to the campsite of Sarah and Abraham? The Bible doesn't tell us. But five chapters and fourteen years later, the Lord visited Sarah. Her life, also, had been burdened and full of trouble. The root of her problem was not fertility, like Hagar's, but infertility.

Once years before, Sarah had laughed sarcastically at messengers who predicted she would have a baby. It seemed a ridiculous thing since she was long past childbearing age. When confronted with the fact that she'd laughed behind closed doors, Sarah denied it (Genesis 18:10–15). But that didn't change the facts. God knew. He is the God-Who-Sees our secrets. In spite of what we try to hide from him, he leads us toward our destiny.

At a ripe old age, Sarah bore a boy named Isaac and laughed again. But this time the sarcasm was gone. This time, it was just fun, hilarity, and real toe-tingling joy. She said right out loud: "God has made me laugh." But the part I like best is when Sarah added, "and everyone who hears about this will laugh with me" (Genesis 21:6). I think God has given women the power to move on in life through the contagion of laughter.

I've spent the past several years collecting quips about laughter and sayings that make me laugh. I have a lot of quotes about dieting, middle age, motherhood, husbands, wrinkles, love — you name it: all those hot spots in a woman's life that would kill us if we let them get us down. The secret is to *not* let them get you down. The secret of not letting them get you down is to laugh about them. In fact, I try to find ways to make the saddest things funny.

We can sigh about things, or we can laugh. Both these responses release pressure, but which is the most fun? We laugh so we won't scream. Laughter is a riotous vote of acceptance that he is the *God-Who-Sees*. Whatever it is probably won't go away, so we might as well live and laugh through it. When we double over laughing, we're bending so we won't break. If you think your particular troubles are too heavy and too traumatic to laugh about, remember that laughing is like changing a baby's diaper. It doesn't solve any problems permanently, but it makes things more acceptable for a while.

You have a choice. Laugh in sarcasm or laugh with joy. Try it both ways, then write and tell me what worked for you!

"Dear Jesus, teach me to laugh; but don't let me forget I cried. Amen."

TRAFFIC BALLET

Marilyn Meberg

But let all who take refuge in you
be glad; let them ever sing for joy.

PSALM 5:11

This morning I was in my kitchen doing the mildly mindless things I do each day between 7 and 8 A.M. Luci had just left, having delivered a grapefruit plucked from her backyard tree only minutes before. (Sometimes I truly think I live in Paradise.) I flipped on *Good Morning, America* to see if they knew anything I should and settled into my final cup of tea.

Am I ever glad I did! There was a segment that caused me to whoop with laughter and delight. I couldn't wait to tell you about it . . . in fact, I didn't even finish that cup of tea! I've dashed to my desk instead. Here's what set me off . . .

They interviewed a guy named Tony from Providence, Rhode Island, who is a traffic cop. He described how neither he nor any of the other guys on the traffic detail could bear one duty each of them had for at least an hour a day. They had to stand in the middle of a busy intersection directing traffic, and he said it was so boring and uneventful he could hardly endure it. He decided to try and spice up that dull task with something that would at least entertain himself and make the hour go faster.

He began experimenting with exaggerated hand and arm movements which led to rhythmically syncopated body swings to go with the movements of his limbs. Finally, after only a few days, he began twirling from left to right, startling drivers with his flourishes of "hurry up," "slow down," or "stop!" That ultimately led to occasionally doing full body spins which culminated in the splits.

Motorists grew to appreciate his antics so much they honked and clapped until he had so many enthusiastic fans it created traffic jams, which only increased his need to twirl, flourish, and point to get cars moving. To avoid the hazards his accumulation of fans presented, Tony was assigned to different intersections each day so no one knew for sure where he'd be performing.

As this interview was going on we, the viewing audience, were treated to a video of Tony's "intersection ballet." Buses and cars were whizzing past in such close proximity to him I wondered if he was ever hit by any of the vehicles. The question was posed to Tony, and he said that he bounced off the side of a moving bus once because he lost his balance during one of his twirls. He said he suffered no bodily harm from the experience but that it did inspire him to do a bit of practicing of his twirls in the basement of his home that night.

What a perfect example Tony is of how to practice a laugh lifestyle. A laugh lifestyle is predicated upon our attitude toward the daily stuff of life. When those tasks seem too dull to endure, figure out a way to make them fun; get creative and entertain yourself. If the stuff of life for you right now is not dull and boring but instead painful and overwhelming, find something in the midst of the pain that makes you smile or giggle anyway. There's always something somewhere . . . even if you have to just pretend to laugh until you really do!

You need that joy break, so take at least one every day. Hey, how about twirling and flourishing in your kitchen, grocery store, or office? It works for Tony!

"We have joy, dear Father, because we can take refuge in you. You provide our safety, our security, our eternal hope. Because of those loving assurances, enable us to see the joy, feel the joy, and even twirl with joy. Thank you that you are our reason for joy each day. Amen."

Why Bother?

Barbara Johnson

We also rejoice in our sufferings,
because we know that suffering
produces perseverance;
perseverance, character;
and character, hope.

ROMANS 5:3–4

Do you ever have those days when everything
in you groans out, "WHY BOTHER?" Why
should I keep on trying . . . why should I
stand up against the high tides of life . . . why
should I stretch to love the unlovely . . . why
should I keep hanging in there when no one
appreciates my efforts and so few even know
the sacrifices I've made . . . why should I put
up with all this?!

I had a day like that recently. Over the holidays last year Bill and I met our son and his
family for a fun gathering outside Seattle.
Everything was going along great until
Christmas night when the whole Northwest

was slammed with an unbelievable ice storm. My plans to get home to Southern California the next day, where I had numerous deadlines to meet (and where it was warm!), went up in icicles.

For four days Bill and I were stuck in a small hotel room, far from where I "needed" to be, and a bit too close to hysteria as we watched two more storms barrel in. In between trips back and forth to the airport (which kept closing just as we'd pull up), I muttered to myself and used the sanity I had left to keep from spewing out my frustration to innocent onlookers — like the airline ticket agents and my husband.

Into my gloom and frustration, God sent a message of hope. In the mail the day before I'd left home, I'd received a tape from a pastor in Ohio whom I didn't even know. I'm not sure why I even plopped it and my Walkman into my suitcase because I have a lot of tapes lying around that I never find time to listen to. But God knew. In a voice full of assurance and victory, this pastor reminded me that "someday, the trumpet will sound and the dead will rise and we will be caught up to meet him in the skies!"

This life is not the end of the story! And my stay in that cramped hotel was oh, so temporary. However discouraged and beat up we may get here on earth, we can have joy in abundance because of what he promises us will be the outcome of our trials: finer character in this world and eternal joy in the next.

We all want the eternal joy part, but maybe you're saying, "Thanks, but no thanks!" to the finer character part. I know that's how I felt as holiday joy turned into post-holiday blues. It's hard not to feel beaten down by life sometimes. Do we really want greater perseverance and Christlike character if it means we have to keep suffering? That kind of deal can really bring out our "Why bother's." But according to the apostle Paul, the chicken can't come before the egg. The character that is refined through the fire of patient suffering is the bedrock of our hope for eternity. As we identify with the sufferings of Christ here on earth, we cultivate within us his passion for reuniting with his Father forevermore. We refuse to get too comfortable in our temporary home and we persevere toward our final destination with the blazing hope of glory. "And hope does not disappoint us" (Romans 5:5).

I can't think of a better foundation on which to build a laugh life-style. When we see things in light of eternity, our "Why bother's?" can become "Why not's?" — and we can plunge into our circumstances with a joy born in heaven.

"God in heaven, remind me that whatever comes into my life comes only with your permission and is designed to make me like your precious Son. Thank you that your grace is sufficient to carry me through every trial on earth, and your love will one day catch me up in glory forevermore. Amen."

Joy, Joy, Joy
. . . Forevermore

Without Conditions

Luci Swindoll

Now when a man works,
his wages are not credited to
him as a gift, but as an obligation.
However, to the man who
does not work but trusts God
who justifies the wicked,
his faith is credited as righteousness.

ROMANS 4:4–5

Here's what I hate: you open up your mailbox, and crammed in with the mail you want to receive is a huge envelope with your name in big letters on the front. *LUCI SWINDOLL, YOU HAVE JUST WON ONE MILLION DOLLARS, CONGRATULATIONS!!!* Inside the envelope is the postscript in little tiny letters: *if your number is called.* Oh, boy! And your immediate thought is, *you can't get something for nothing.*

Or how 'bout this: you open your mail and staring you in the face is an opportunity to fly free. *Oh, wow . . . free!* Then you read on: ". . . if you will just open a credit card account with American Express." Well, okay. So you open the account. Your free ticket comes in the mail, and on it you read: *Certain conditions apply . . . please see other side.* And the conditions? Well, in order to use this particular ticket which is non-negotiable, non-transferable, and non-refundable, you must fly on a Tuesday night only, between the hours of 11 P.M. and 2 A.M., sitting only in a middle seat, with no carry-on luggage, on a flight going east only, with four stops on the way to Paducah, Kentucky. And your immediate thought is, *you can't get something for nothing.*

Or, here's a good one: you find a flyer under your windshield wiper. One night in a resort hotel is yours . . . absolutely free. No cost. No obligation. No restriction. However . . . the free night must follow ten consecutive nights in that same room in that same hotel. And your immediate thought is — you got it, *you can't get something for nothing.*

Then, you pick up your New Testament and turn to Ephesians 2:8–9, and there in bold print you read these comforting words: "For it is by grace you have been saved, through faith — and this not from yourselves, it is the gift of God — not by works, so that no one can boast."

The wonderful thing about the Christian life is that we all enter freely. No matter who you are, where you're from, what your experience has been, Jesus Christ invites you to freely come. No conditions. No restrictions. No small print. No waiting. About this, you can be certain.

My favorite theological doctrine is that of "justification." It is the sovereign act of God whereby he declares the believing sinner righteous, while still in a sinning state. In other words, when a person comes to God, just as she is — while still in her sinning state — God looks at her and because of what Jesus Christ did on the cross he proclaims her righteous. She does not have to clean up her act. She does not have to do penance. She does not have to be thin or good-looking or rich or famous or accomplished. All she has to do is believe God for the forgiveness of her sins.

If you have never made the wonderful discovery of knowing Christ personally, you can do so at this very moment. Know that God loves you unconditionally; know that Christ died on the cross to pay the penalty for your sins; know that upon your invitation he will come into your life, forgive your sins, and begin a personal relationship with you. There is no waiting. Once you place your faith in him, you can be sure that you have eternal life. In fact, he is preparing a place for your comfort, every consecutive night for all eternity.

Salvation is a gift. He gives. You receive. Pray a simple prayer like this:

"Lord Jesus, I need you. I want to know you personally. Thank you for dying on the cross for my sins. I open the door of my life and receive you as my Savior and Lord. Thank you for forgiving me and giving me eternal life. Take control of my life and make me the kind of person you want me to be. Amen."

WOMEN OF FAITH

Joy Breaks is based on the popular Women of Faith conferences. Women of Faith is partnering with Zondervan Publishing House, Integrity Music, *Today's Christian Woman* magazine, and Campus Crusade to offer conferences, publications, worship music, inspirational gifts that support and encourage today's Christian women.

Since their beginning in January of 1996, the Women of Faith conferences have enjoyed an enthusiastic welcome by women across the country. Women of Faith conference plans presently extend through the year 2000. Call 1-888-49-FAITH for the many conference locations and dates available.

www.women-of-faith.com